P⚡WERLight Lit
Tips for Better Teaching

by Tonja K. Taylor

POWERLight Learning
Fort Worth, Texas

And you shall teach them to your children, speaking of them when you sit in your house and when you walk along the road, when you lie down and when you rise up. - Deut. 11:19, AMPC

Ebook ISBN: **978-1-965641-18-7**

Print Book ISBN: **978-1-965641-21-7**

*A portion of the income from these books (after the tithe) goes to
support organizations throughout the world that **promote the Good
News of Jesus Christ our LORD the King!***

Scripture quotations taken from the New American Standard
Bible® (NASB), Copyright © 1960, 1962, 1963, 1968, 1971, 1972,
1973, 1975, 1977, 1995 by The Lockman Foundation. Used by
permission. www.Lockman.org[1].

Scripture quotations taken from the Amplified® Bible (AMP),
Copyright © 2015 by The Lockman Foundation. Used by permission.
www.Lockman.org[2].

Scripture quotations marked TPT are from The Passion
Translation®. Copyright © 2017, 2018 by Passion & Fire Ministries,
Inc. Used by permission. All rights reserved.
ThePassionTranslation.com.

Tonja K. Taylor has a mandate to teach others through books,
presentations, online courses, and more, to help them experience the
love, power, and creativity of Christ. She has enjoyed many
God-breathed adventures from teaching and championing kids for over
40 years, in church, schools, community organizations in the USA, and
online in eight other countries.

---

1. http://www.Lockman.org

2. http://www.Lockman.org

Her experiences in ministry, business, education, and the fine arts allow her to bring a multi-faceted approach to her work, so that her audiences are engaged, enriched, and empowered as they learn—providing them with an amazing amount of value for their investment. Also, Tonja and her heroic husband live to glorify LORD Jesus, our soon-returning King!

See the back of the book for a list of many of her other works, and read Tonja's **1,250+ articles on the FaithWriters.com** site: **https://www.faithwriters.com/member-profile.php?id=64826.** Many of the articles in this book are reprinted from FaithWriters.com.

Our **YouTube channels** are **"River Rain Creative"** (This channel was truncated years ago (not by Tonja), and includes an audio version of some books): https://www.youtube.com/@riverraincreative599 and also the more recent **"POWERLight Learning":** https://www.youtube.com/channel/ UCwH6SsQESk-mU77azYaj6zw/videos (This is most recent, because I could not upload anymore to the River Rain Creative channel, for some reason. POWERLight Learning will be expanded later this spring and beyond.)

Listen to Tonja's multi-subject **"RainWater" podcasts on Apple:** https://podcasts.apple.com/ca/podcast/rain-water/id146070928. (Updated works coming soon!)

Help students understand their rights on campus: **https://www.youtube.com/watch?v=WfFZsX2aW80** Also, enjoy the other YouTube links in the book for some articles.

Thank You To Teachers Everywhere

To my dear husband (who served cumulatively as a teacher in public schools for almost 20 years), and to all dedicated educators: thank you for caring enough about your service as a teacher (in public or private schools; in church or community; online; at home; or in any capacity) to invest your time (and money, if you purchased it) in reading this book. May it inspire you to be more free, bold, and thankful at the opportunities the LORD has given you to influence many lives—which will influence many other lives.

Even if you think you've never served to "teach" anyone in an official capacity, remember that every person is truly an "influencer"—for others are always watching us, whether we realize it or not, and our lives affect them.

May we yield daily to the Master Teacher, Jesus Christ the LORD, and be the teachers, the influencers, the ambassadors that He died for us to be!

So we are Christ's ambassadors, God making His appeal as it were through us. We [as Christ's personal representatives] beg you for His sake to lay hold of the divine favor [now offered you] *and* be reconciled to God. - 2 Corinthians 5:20, AMPC

(Note From Tonja:
Some of these articles, which were almost all published previously on FaithWriters.com, may share some of the same material.

As I used to tease my dear daughter (now 28 and happily married for 5 years to her best friend of 15 years, bless the LORD) when I homeschooled her in her 6th and 7th grade, "Repetition's how we learn. Repetition's how we learn. Repetition's how—"

"Mommmmm!" she'd say, and look a bit annoyed.

So, just like our students, we haven't always caught things the first time. So there you go.☺)

Table Of Contents

Why We Can Be Effective Teachers

https://www.youtube.com/watch?v=Acmelx55FDU
[Not in your own strength] for it is God Who is all the while effectually at work in you [energizing and creating in you the power and desire], both to will and to work for His good pleasure *and* satisfaction *and* delight. – Phil. 2:13, AMPC

We can be effective teachers for several reasons. Here are several things I've done and do. If you have done or do these, they will help you be more effective.

First, I believe in prayer, and I pray for each student and session. That does not make me perfect, of course, but I truly believe God helps me, because He loves every child, and His love and wisdom flow through me.

Second, I have many years' experience in teaching many things, to many individuals and groups, in many situations. This gives me multi-faceted experience and skills, plus confidence in my abilities (with my confidence first being in God helping me (Eph. 2:10; Phil. 2:13 and 4:13), and I have many pieces of "love art" from students, as well as kudos from supervisors and parents in my brick-and-mortar schools and from my online schools, to prove it. ☺

Third, I connect quickly with my students to discover their interests, and I use various techniques and strategies to help them understand whatever concept I'm teaching, changing angles and examples as needed, until they get it.

Fourth, I have a lot of positive energy, a big smile, and high expectations for my students, while allowing for "life," and changing circumstances.

Fifth, I quickly admit it when I'm wrong, tell the kids I can learn from them, and congratulate them when they are honest about not knowing something.

Sixth, I'm not going to stop teaching—in one way or another (and, truly, writing is another form of teaching!)—until I go to Heaven, and who knows? I may be teaching then! (It has been stated by more than one highly regarded minister that what we weave in this life, we will wear for eternity.)

Seventh, the kids can tell quickly that I care about them and their success.

All of these can be possible for you. Also, you can ask the LORD for more strategies for success, and He will supply. He loves you, and every student and family you touch!

7 Affirmations for Students

I don't remember if I told my fourth-graders in the small rural public school that the affirmations I had them say every morning were based on the Bible. I think it would have been a blessing to most of those sweeties, if they'd known that, but it may have created some problems with the administration.

However, almost every one of my students immediately loved doing this as a class, and most wanted to lead. I would have them stand, and, after we said the "Pledge of Allegiance", I would stand and lead them in the "Daily Affirmations" God had given me for them.

My order of operations was that, during the nine weeks, every student would lead the class (even if they didn't want to; I'd let another student with whom they were friends stand with them if needed), usually several times.

Sometimes, a student would try to be funny, and say them too quickly, or in a high-pitched voice. It was a distraction, so when that happened, I'd have them start again. It didn't take long for the other kids to tell the distracting students to "Shut up!" and then we'd start again.

This is what the LORD led me to have them say:

Using my power of choice,
I control myself.
I show respect to myself and others.
I am wise, so I obey my leaders.
I am excellent.
I am trustworthy.
I am quick to help others.
I am special and loved, and I believe it.

All of these are based on the Word of God! I believe, because our Father God is so good, so all-knowing, so eager to bless us, that His Spirit overshadowed these words when my students spoke them in unison. I could see the heart in almost all of my students, every morning, as they said them. A couple were reluctant on some days—but they were still hearing them, and thus, those good seeds were being planted, and watered!

Another thing about the Word of God is that, once it's rooted in the heart, it remains! During the last few months of the year, my word processing program that worked with the interactive whiteboard was never repaired, even though I requested it. So, I came in one day and could not project the affirmations, as I had been doing for months, for the class to read.

However, a few students jumped up and eagerly volunteered to lead the class from memory! I was so blessed, and close to tears, as I saw and heard their eager hearts to lead their classmates in those inspiring words, with no writing on the board—for the affirmations were written in their hearts! Glory to God!

The LORD is so very faithful! He always puts His blessing on our genuine efforts to help others, even if they don't show appreciation. After all, He says in His Word that, when we do it to the "least of these," or "the littlest one," that we do it for Him. Praise Him, our good and kind and gracious, merciful, faithful Master Who loves us so much He died for us!

Ask the LORD today for strategies to draw your class or family closer to Christ. He will help you!

Here is the link to a writing the LORD gave me, which I meant as a "positive" alternative to normal discipline writing assignments: **https://www.youtube.com/watch?v=zCEaASFhGto**

I was amazed at how God worked through this to touch and change my students!

Ways to Strengthen Relationships

He that loveth pureness of heart, for the grace of his lips the king shall be his friend.—Prov. 22:11, KJV

Excellent communication to the glory of God among people is always His plan.

Our students and families need to know they are important to us, and not just on parent-teacher nights, nor just during class time.

The LORD inspired me this morning to send a list of three learning resources (that are free, overall) to all my online students, with a short note reminding them I'm on vacation the first week of January, and blessings for a happy New Year.

It was a little but meaningful gift to them, and, I bet, a delightful surprise to get this email from me. It shows I'm thinking of them, even outside of school hours.

(By the way, I also tell my students during our first session, or within the first few, that I pray for them daily, and I also pray for the LORD to help me help them. I haven't had any of them yet act scornful about that, even if they are openly of a different religion. Of course, true Christianity is not a religion, but a relationship with the living God, Jesus Christ the LORD! Hallelujah!)

I've used some of these resources during tutoring sessions with my students, but there is a lot to explore.

Parents are busy, and many of my students don't get online outside of school time without their parents, but by sending these resources, I'm believing this will help the parents allow their students to get on these sites and learn, and perhaps even share a bit of time discussing some of these concepts with them.

By the way, here are the sites I suggested, all with totally or mostly free resources for learning:

https://www.ixl.com/ (10 free questions in each subject per day! Very generous of them! can get a lot of practice daily, just from the freebies, and the subscription prices is very reasonable.)

http://www.kahnacademy.org[1]

http://www.quizlet.com[2] (Free or subscription)

There are many more, but these can keep your student(s) positively productive!

Train up a child in the way he should go: and when he is old, he will not depart from it.—Proverbs 22:6, KJV

---

1.   http://www.kahnacademy.org/
2.   http://www.quizlet.com/

"Thank You!" Can Help Build Relationships

What is it people want the most? (That can truly be another essay, although I can make a reference to the LORD in this).

What is it *GOD* wants the most?

What most people want at their core is to be recognized and appreciated.

Study after study, survey after survey, proves that we humans, unlike animals, crave appreciation.

And how much more does God—although He is so very good to us all, whether we ever acknowledge or thank Him or not!

44But I tell you, Love your enemies and pray for those who persecute you, 45To show that you are the children of your Father Who is in heaven; for He makes His sun rise on the wicked and on the good, and makes the rain fall upon the upright and the wrongdoers [alike]. - Matthew 5:44-45, AMPC

Truly, He above all is worthy of our expressions of gratitude! In fact, it is a prerequisite for entering His presence.

(The ultimate prerequisite, of course, in communing with God is being born again and wearing the robe of righteousness because one is covered by the blood of Jesus shed on the cross. But what I speak of here is worship, relating to, communicating with, the King of Heaven, our Daddy God.)

In Psalm 100, the LORD says, **"Enter His gates with thanksgiving, and enter His courts with praise."**

(In other words, we can't even get in the GATE, we can't even BEGIN to have fellowship with God until we are THANKFUL for all He's done!

We do not like to hear our students complain, and in fact, we do not tolerate it, or at least not for long—because it sets a bad example for the rest, and can disrupt the class.

We really like it when our students (and biological children!) are polite by saying "Thank you," but not all of them have been taught to be thankful. What a sad thing! So, we can affirm and commend those students who do know how to do thankful, and be examples to them, hoping they will catch those manners and practice them.

We can strengthen their gratefulness in other ways: (1) By helping them to make a list (working in buddies or small groups, if needed) of things they are thankful for, as I did for a Thanksgiving holiday craft (and which inspired and delighted the kids; so much so that they all did 100, and one boy up to 200!), and (2) helping them unite to help others less fortunate (and I was so touched when my precious students—several of whom were living in unfortunate conditions themselves—wanted to buy cans of food to send to children in an orphanage in Mexico that I told them about!); and (3) write thank you cards.

The Thanksgiving-time-capsule-lists that I had them write were a form of thank you cards, by the way.

That brings me to this: You can strengthen relationships with your own child(s) teacher, and certainly with the parents of your students, by sending thank you cards!

One cool way the LORD showed me, that strengthened my relationships with both students and their parents, was to write short hand-written notes on brightly colored paper, and send it home with the students. (I wrote in cursive to save time, and although all the students were delighted, some had to ask me to "interpret" it, for they had not been taught to read cursive writing. But that was just a chance to reaffirm them even more, as they heard me read my words of thankfulness and other affirmations out loud to them. Hallelujah!)

God has helped me strengthen many, many relationships by using this simple but powerful tool of saying "Thank you" for years and years, and have joyfully surprised many people; from leaders in business, to many parents at different schools, by sending a simple card; giving them recognition and appreciation.

As a Believer, I've made it a practice to also include a Scripture or two as the LORD leads in almost all thank-you cards I've sent through the years. I've had some people who received them tell me that no one had ever sent them a thank you card before, and I've had others say that my words were exactly what they needed.

So, go for it. Any way that you model and express the power of thanksgiving to and in front of your students, can only strengthen your relationships with them and their families.

29Do you see a man diligent *and* skillful in his business? He will stand before kings; he will not stand before obscure men. – Prov. 22:29, AMPC

Use Genesis 50:20 With Your Students

As for you, you thought evil against me, but God meant it for good, to bring about that many people should be kept alive, as they are this day.—Genesis 50:20, AMPC

When one of my students cursed and said other things with which I didn't agree (OMG, etc.), the LORD gave me a neat strategy to turn these into a positive!

This was a junior high student, but this can be used with any age.

Here's the simple, turn-this-to-positive (which is the hallmark of our awesome God; Jesus came to destroy the works of the devil (I John 3:8), and to work good out of the devil's mess! Hallelujah!)—

Every time he cursed or said something else that was slurring God's name (although I don't think he meant it; he'd just picked it up as slang, etc.), I would exclaim, "God is GOOD—ALL the time!" He was not (yet) a Believer, but he knew I was, for he'd asked me directly, and I had replied that yes, I certainly believe in and follow Jesus Christ!

He actually laughed (in a respectful) way. So, instead of being religious and legalistic, the LORD Who loves him helped us both have a good time, being aware of the difference of thought, but overcoming any negatives with blessed positives—as only the LORD can do, and as He points out in 2 Timothy 2:24-26!

24[1] And the Lord's servant must not be quarrelsome but kind to everyone, able to teach, patiently enduring evil, 25[2] correcting his opponents with gentleness. God may perhaps grant them repentance leading to a knowledge of the truth, 26[3] and they may come to their senses and escape from the snare of the devil, after being captured by him to do his will.—2 Timothy 2:24-26, ESV

He poured Grace upon my lips! Hallelujah!

---

1.   http://biblehub.com/2_timothy/2-24.htm

2.   http://biblehub.com/2_timothy/2-25.htm

3.   http://biblehub.com/2_timothy/2-26.htm

All my students (whom are all online now, for the past three years) know that I pray for them daily. I tell them so. Even when I was teaching public school, I'd tell them I loved them, and prayed, and sometimes I prayed in the classroom. I was aware I might be disciplined for that, but I never was, and the students loved it.

The LORD is The Master Teacher, and the Father of all our students. He will continue to help us with divine and effective strategies to model right behavior to our students, and help them know we love God, we love them, and we and He are for them. Amen!

And we know that in all things God works for the good of those who love him, who have been called according to his purpose.—Romans 8:28

Using Bloom's Taxonomy to Teach Students

Each of these describes a level of Bloom's Taxonomy (remembering, understanding, applying, analyzing, evaluating, and creating, with creating being the top level). This particular example can be effective for upper elementary students:

Name of Story: "Goldilocks and the Three Bears"

apply/demonstrate/illustrate (3.Application)

What could Goldilocks could have done instead of tasting the soup and sleeping in the beds of the three bears?

evaluate/rate/defend (6.Evaluation)

What do you think would have happened if the bears had been home when Goldilocks arrived?

list/recognize/recall (1. Knowledge)

How many bowls of soup did she taste, and whose beds did she sleep in?

analyze/compare/distinguish (4.Analysis)

What did she say about the soups that she tasted?

construct/organize/propose (5.Synthesis)

What do you think would have happened if she got to the bears' house while they were there and she asked them if she could taste their soups and sleep in their beds?

describe/explain/restate (2.Comprehension)

What were the names of the three bears and were they happy that Goldilocks visited and tasted their soups and slept in their beds?

This example can help you understand more about Bloom's and how to utilize it to help your students!

2 Quick Ideas to Help Struggling Readers

Train up a child in the way he should go [and in keeping with his individual gift or bent], and when he is old he will not depart from it.—Proverbs 22:6, AMPC

My husband, who was himself a band director for 15 years and who worked with preschoolers for 4 years, had some great ideas to help my ELA students (Great ideas, my Beloved!):

(1) Let them bring their favorite book to share with the class

(2) Encourage them to read every day, not just the five days I teach them

I told my sweet lower elementary students his suggestions today, and they were delighted! They are at home, receiving my tutoring online, so a couple of them immediately ran and got their books and started sharing. It was adorable.

However, I gently reminded them that today was Tuesday, and the share session would be Thursday. This will be their Blessing for the week, and I will also share (as they have asked) one of my books, which will include my daughter's art.

I love the way God works in these wonderful ways! This share time will be very helpful to them, to increase their understanding about titles, predictions, authors, illustrators, and other parts of a book, while also improving their fluency, comprehension, and presentation skills.

In addition, as I told my darling husband, this is a subtle but powerful seed we're planting in them about the unity of our marriage, and our love for them.

How awesome is our God—the perfect Teacher and Father of all! JESUS IS LORD!

10 Tips to Help Students Be Better Readers

Our inner selves wait [earnestly] for the Lord; He is our Help and our Shield.—Psalm 33:20, AMPC

I have used these tips in public school, and online, in various combinations, to help readers enjoy reading and grow in their skills and confidence. God wants to help every student be a better reader, and these are strategies He's given me, that I learned from someone else, or with which He personally inspired me. I know they can help your reader(s) be stronger and more confident readers, too!

(**1**) Allow the reader to choose a book that appeals to them. There is great power and confidence in being free to choose.

(**2**) If it is too difficult, you can assign a "reading buddy"—a more confident and skilled reader—to read the work out loud the first time (or at least part of it). This will allow the less-skilled reader to hear the text, including correct articulation, pitch, pauses for punctuation, etc.

(**3**) If it is too easy, let the reader grow in confidence as he or she reads it to a buddy, or even better (if there's time, although it's a great thing to make time, like on Friday afternoons, etc.), to the class, family, friends, or whomever will listen (Grandmas and Grandpas are excellent at this!). ells

(**4**) Things can often sound differently to our brains than when we read silently, so have your student(s) read out loud as often as possible; in school, at home, etc. You can have them "whisper read," which is literally whispering, but it's still out-loud reading, that their brains can hear.

(**5**) Have them write their opinions, questions, or other thoughts about what they've read. You can have them look at a cover of a book or an illustration for a story, and predict what they think the story is about, before they read it. Then follow up and discuss it after the reading(s).

(6) Allow them to draw pictures or write thoughts, while they listen to others read. I used to think this was a distraction, but many, like myself and my daughter, prefer to take notes and/or draw pictures, and are truly activity listening! (Now my daughter is an accomplished artist, and has her four-year university degree in commercial art, as well as her own online business selling her art. She has also drawn some interesting art while in church, and many pictures that I have kept in my treasure box.)

(7) Gradually increase the difficulty, or "level," of books for each reader. Wean those students who are ready, or mature enough, away from picture books, to books with just a few pictures—until they are reading chapter books. Chapter books usually only have pictures on the covers, and not inside.

You can find the proper level(s) for your student(s) by checking the Lexile and ATOS numbers. The Lexile level assesses the complexity of the text, so it can be matched with the reader's level, and the ATOS number guides the reader to books that are considered most appropriate for their reading levels.

These are matched with the core standards for students, which is very important to teachers, and often, to parents.

(8) Pray for your reader(s) daily—and let them know you are praying! When I taught in public schools (as a sub, then as a full-time teacher) and told my students I prayed for them daily, it greatly encouraged them, and helped strengthen our relationship. When a student trusts the leader, they are more confident that they can overcome their struggles—reading and otherwise—and the LORD gets the glory.

(9) Have friendly competitions, such as reading the most books, and doing book reports to turn in. The LORD gave me the idea for "P.O.W.E.R. (Purposeful Operations With Eternal Rewards) Readers,"

for my fourth-grade English class, and the student who read the most books during a week would get to wear the crown. They had to turn in book reports of a page long, so I'd have proof that they really read the book(s). They enjoyed that.

When I taught K5 at a Christian school, I would have the kids write out Scriptures and memorize them, or read them out loud to me, and when they did a certain number, they got to choose a prize (which I bought with my own money) from the "store." They loved it, and I'm thankful I was able to help them hide more of the Word of God in their hearts!

(As well-respected ministers have stated, children don't have a "junior Holy Spirit. They have The Holy Spirit," and I know that, when I received my first Bible at age 7, the LORD helped me start understanding it. I received Christ Jesus as my Savior two years later, and He started really helping me understand the Bible! I led my own daughter to Christ Jesus at age 5 (Hallelujah!), and she loved the Bible and church so much! The Word dwells in her richly today!)

(10) Have them write letters to others, and lists of thing to be thankful for. The LORD gave me both of these ideas for that same fourth-grade class. The kids loved them.

The kids were excited that I gave them each a nice glass bottle (Yep. I did have a couple drop theirs, but no one got hurt, and I replaced them quickly.), plus stickers and markers so they could decorate their "Thanksgiving Time Capsules."

They did in November that year, just before Thanksgiving weekend. I required 100 things to write that they were thankful for, and one student hit 100 and wanted to keep going. His list included 200 things expressing his gratitude! Hallelujah!).

They enjoyed the writing (a few struggled with writing 100 things, but their classmates helped them) and the reading out loud, so it was a win-win (as the inspirations of the LORD always are!)!

They were tickled to take them home to their families for Thanksgiving weekend, and a couple were telling other teachers about them.

I also let them share many of the things they were thankful for out loud, in class, so that was more reading and speaking practice.

In addition, I taught them how to write a formal letter (headings and closings and all), with realia—they wrote greetings and encouragements, and even drew sweet pictures, to dear Spanish orphans at a children's home directed by some minister friends in Mexico. I taught them a couple of Spanish words, and they were thrilled about that, too.

My heart was blessed because many of my students wanted to collect cans of food to send them! So precious! So, I explained that people could donate money online—but that the best gift would be for my students to pray for them, and to share their loving letters and art with the children. After a few months, our class got an envelope in the mail, with some replies (a mix of Spanish and English, which our friends were teaching these dear little ones) and darling drawings. So that made quite an impact on both groups!

These tips can help your readers in many ways, whether in school or at home. Of course, the ultimate reading material is the Bible, and there are many versions—even illustrated ones—that are very appealing to children. The sooner they read His Word, the likelier they are to come to Christ at a young age, and grow greatly in their respect for the Word! They and we can never have too much of the Word of God. His Word is life!

1 In the beginning [before all time] was the Word (Christ), and the Word was with God, and the Word was God Himself. 2 He was present originally with God. 3 All things were made and came into existence through Him; and without Him was not even one thing made that has come into being. 4 In Him was Life, and the Life was the Light of men. 5 And the Light shines on in the darkness, for

the darkness has never overpowered it [put it out or absorbed it or appropriated it, and is unreceptive to it].—John 1:1-5, AMPC

20 Success Strategies for Your P.O.W.E.R. Readers

https://www.youtube.com/watch?v=JYgh_LYUDFM (My apologies; title is misspelled!)

Do you see someone skilled in their work? They will serve before kings;—Proverbs 22:29, NIV

I have many hours towards a Masters of Arts in Education, and over 30 years' experience teaching. But you don't have to have these to help your students be a P.O.W.E.R Reader! (Purposeful Operations With Eternal Rewards) Reader!

So what is a P.O.W.E.R. Reader?

It is a reader who knows strategies for success in "Purposeful Operations With Eternal Rewards"!

(This is a term the LORD gave me years ago for my book series, *The Adventures of Princess Pearl, P.O.W.E.R. Girl!* I've retitled the series *P.O.W.E.R. Girl Adventures*. Books 1-5 are complete and will very soon be available, and books 6-8 are in the works!)

P.O.W.E.R. Readers learn and effectively utilize strategies for success, not only in educational pursuits, but in life. Hallelujah!

Your readers—whether it's your child at home, or a class full of "struggling" students (which, from my years of experience, don't struggle nearly as much, when they are given the proper attention and other support!)—can benefit from these simple strategies.

Not only can they gain confidence and positive thinking with the truly helpful tips, but you can sow the Word of God into them!

The LORD has taught me, even in the past couple of years, to say, "LORD, I yield to You. You are the Master Teacher, Jesus, and You created these children and know exactly what they need. I open my mouth and ask that You fill it; that You give me the tongue of the learned; that You cause them to not be able to resist the intelligence and inspiration of Your Spirit, by which I will speak. In Your Name and thank You! Amen."

So here are 20 strategies you can use (or may already be using, at least in some ways), to help give your students excellent success:

1. Start them reading on positive things, not just educational things, and preferably openly inspiring about God. Take all the liberty you have—and make some! "The earth is the LORD's and the fullness thereof, and all the peoples therein," states Psalm 24:1 in God's Word.

Do not fear to use Christian works to share with your students. For instance, when I taught Piano Lab to about 350 5 and 6 graders (averaging 85 or so every 9 weeks) at a large public middle school, I added plenty of hymns to the sheet music mix. They were allowed to choose what they wanted to learn to play, and most of them chose at least one hymn!

I also use a large percentage of Christian works when I teach English Language Arts (ELA) to my online students. The platforms for which I teach explicitly state in the contract(s) that, as a tutor, I have complete freedom to use whatever materials I deem appropriate. The LORD opened my eyes to this one day, and inspired me to use more blatantly Christian materials. After all, this world is crazy, the kids are often at a disadvantage, and we true Believers have the Answer—Jesus Christ, the Living Word!

I often use poems, stories, articles, songs, etc., about God when I teach small groups (1:10) online as I go into public schools, which I'm doing through June this year. I even have them read some of my works, and tell them how the LORD inspired me to write the poem, or story, etc. I remind them that, if I can write a poem at age 10 and have it published and even earn money (True—in 1976, for Grit Magazine!)

So go for it! The LORD's got your back, and He will guide you.

2. Have your students write three or more positive sentences about themselves, then read them out loud. If they can't think of anything, you help them, i.e.: "Mara learns quickly. She is very respectful. She is creative and helpful!" Have them read those things out loud, but, of course, to put "I" in place of their names. We want them to make this as personal as possible. However, most of us enjoy hearing our names, so if they are having more fun speaking their names out loud instead of "I", then good for them!

(Whatever works, as long as all are safe and positive, right? Right!)

Not only will the physical and physiological act of writing benefit them, but focusing on good things about themselves and reading them out loud will affirm their identity and confidence.

(We adults benefit from such, too. After all, we are God's kids (when we truly have received Christ Jesus, His Son, as our LORD and Savior, of course! **But God shows *and* clearly proves His [own] love for us by the fact that while we were still sinners, Christ (the Messiah, the Anointed One) died for us.** – Romans 5:8, AMPC). Hallelujah!

When I taught fourth grade math and English—where the lunches were 100% free, because of the rate of poverty in the area—I would have the students say 7 short affirmations out loud as a group (in unison, which is very powerful for many reasons), first thing every morning. The students were eager to lead.

When my electronic whiteboard went out (and the school refused to repair it, for some reason!), I was so blessed! The kids had memorized these affirmations in their hearts, and they continued to take turns leading their peers to say them every morning, even without seeing them on the board. Hallelujah!

3. Teach them to look for a tiny real word in the big unfamiliar word. Make it a treasure hunt! Often, they will find one, like "cat" in "categorize," and "our" in "devoured," and the smaller word hidden in the big one will help them with the pronunciation; sometimes, with the meaning. One example of the latter is "repeatedly," where it's easy for the students to spot "repeat" as the root word, and then infer what "repeatedly" means.

4. Remember that almost every word in English must have at least one vowel in every syllable/beat. (A couple of exceptions, as my dear, detail-oriented husband pointed out, are "schism" and "prism".) To help the students understand the number of syllables/beats in words, especially unfamiliar, longer words, I clap my hands so they can hear and see it. Have them repeat the word until they get it right, in pronunciation—including the right stress on the right syllable(s).

As Harry Wong is often quoted, "Teachers are the sculptors of the human race."

I agree, but God said it first: **"Train up a child in the way he should go [and in keeping with his individual gift or bent], and when he is old he will not depart from it."**—Proverbs 22:6, AMPC

Go for it. The kids need you, and God will help you! You can do this!

Now, let's get started with Strategies 5-8!

5. Most words with the "ed" suffix blend into the syllable before them, i.e., "walked," but a few have the "ed" pronounced as its own syllable (i.e., "blended"). You must teach them about prefixes (which have the power to change the meanings of the root word) and suffixes (which have the power to change the part of speech of a word), and that the "ed" suffix can either blend with the one before it to produce one sound, or have a distinct sound. These words are forms of sight words, and they will learn them the more they see them. Having a list of both types would be helpful.

6. Many words from other languages have been incorporated into English. Examples are "zephyr" (a soft spring breeze), and one of my favorites, "*objet d'art*," which is a French word that means "masterpiece" or "work of art."

My students enjoy me telling them they are each an "*objet d'art*" (ob zha dar, or ob zha duh, but of course I prefer the first pronunciation, because the second one sounds like I'm calling them "dumb" or something negative at the end!), and it's an easy way to build the relationship. Also, I tell them my dad used to joke that "French people spell funny," (True!) and that words like "ballet," and "bouquet" also come from that language, but of course are not pronounced like they look.

I also like to teach them "mariposa," the Spanish name for butterfly, and have them read the poem the LORD gave me (I've included it as one of the three bonuses at the end of the book.).

It includes the name of "Elohim," which is Hebrew for "The Godhead," and "The Creator."

These simple things have sparked some very interesting conversations about the LORD, even if it was just a sentence or two. God can water and bring great increase on even the smallest seed planted to His glory!

Many words in our language are not phonetically spelled, like "knee, knight, know," and "gnat, gnaw" and "light, laugh, fought," and more. But you can have fun with it. Like I've told many English language learners—native to the USA or not—I can't explain English, I just teach it!

That gives them a good laugh, and helps them relax more. When they relax, they are more receptive and learn more easily—like us adults often do!

7. Using context clues—dialogue, descriptions, and actions of the characters in fiction, and information (along with pictures)—to infer (deduce; figure out) the meaning of new words is very important. Students should learn early how to use a dictionary, but using context clues is even more important, because a dictionary, online or hard copy, and other people to ask, are not always available.

Having them practice using context clues in various ways is an extremely valuable skill they will need in school, college, and beyond. I like to remind them that, when they have their own business, or are working in any field and their supervisor asks them to learn material and then report to him or her, or a group, they will need to use context clues to help them infer things more quickly. I also tell them that, even if they are reading a new book for pleasure, they can use context clues so they don't have to look up something on their phone(s) or ask!

It is important to plant seeds of higher thinking, to help them "look beyond what they see" and set big goals for the future! God will give you lots of neat ways to do that!

8. Predicting and previewing—Having the students look at the title of a book, and the cover or illustration, and predict what they think will happen will help them focus, and stimulate their creativity. You can also praise them when they get it right, or even close. You could even use a book with a Bible story, as the Holy Spirit leads, especially if it has pictures, for elementary kids.

After reading a book, you can affirm their correct guesses and otherwise commend them as appropriate.

Train up a child in the way he should go; even when he is old he will not depart from it.—Proverbs 22:6, ESV

Let's continue, with strategies 9-12:

9. While the student reads the text or poem, be ready to help them right then to repeat the words they mispronounce—immediately. Correct the mispronunciation, then have the student read the sentence again, speaking the word(s) correctly.

Some teachers advise to wait till the end of the paragraph. It's your choice. I have found that it works better for my students when I correct them as they are reading, then have them read again.

All the class is hearing it—the correction(s) being made, and the correct reading. (They also know I am paying extremely close attention, which helps psychologically to strengthen the positive relationship.)

10. If a student has been reading intensely for several sentences, and having a hard time with many words, then another student can read for a while. If the second student has as much difficulty, then the text may be too hard for the class, especially if you are teaching a small group. As good teachers, we must adjust as needed to benefit each student, as much as possible. If the text seems to be too hard for the class, the teacher should read it slowly first, and remind the students the word will "stretch" them.

11. It is also good to have a stronger, more confident reader to read some, and to help the students whose skills are not as developed. Putting the kids in pairs, with a stronger reader helping a weaker one, is a good idea. Let them read the text for the class out loud to each other, and then work to persuade the weaker reader of the pair to present it to the class. This will build their confidence and skill. Allow the stronger reader to prompt/help the weaker one, as the weaker one reads aloud. One P.O.W.E.R Reader can help beget another!

12. Finding subjects the students enjoy reading is good, but they also need to be introduced to a few works they may never think to choose. Inspirational and fascinating scientific things, along with tastefully humorous works or poetry, are good choices.

There are 8 more strategies for success for your P.O.W.E.R Readers following this, so check them out!

Also remember, as Philippians 4:13 (AMPC) states: **"I have strength for all things in Christ Who empowers me [I am ready for anything and equal to anything through Him Who infuses inner strength into me; I am self-sufficient in Christ's sufficiency]."**

Hallelujah! Go for it! God is with you, and helping you to help your students be P.O.W.E.R Readers!

Now, let's look at strategies 13-16:

13. Having a good selection of different books and kids' magazines, along with higher-level books and magazines (which will be mentally and emotionally safe for the children to read, of course!) is a good plan.

They don't have to be blatantly about God, but every time I've bought books and magazines to donate to my public school class libraries and other places where the children can choose, what I've found is that they are surprised and delighted to find books about God!

The little ones comes from God, and they are usually hungry to learn more about Him. Hallelujah!

14. If a child chooses a book or magazine to read and quickly puts it down, it may be that the student finds it too hard, instead of boring. You can ask them questions to ascertain the case.

15. Some books have the ATOS (reading) levels listed, and you can gauge what would usually be right for your child's grade. Otherwise, you can type phrases like "4th grade reading lists" or whatever grade your child is in, and links will be brought up for you to choose from. Also, remember that, in summer, the student is headed for the next grade, so it's good to have a mix of books from the past year, and several at a higher level.

16. Teach them the SQ3R (Survey, Question, Vocab/Box/Color, Read) method—important for 4th grade and up. They may not comprehend why they are doing it, but just teaching them to use this strategy will help them more than they can know at this age.

Remember, the LORD will guide you to guide your child to the best. After all, He created you, your children, your students, and He loves them more than you do!

The Lord appeared from of old to me [Israel], saying, **Yes, I have loved you with an everlasting love; therefore with loving-kindness have I drawn you and continued My faithfulness to you.**—Jeremiah 31:3, AMPC

Here are the remaining strategies, 17-20:

17. If they are shy about reading, you can ask them to "whisper read" to themselves, as you (or a stronger reader) read out loud. They may warm up and decide they want to read.

Sometimes, they may be overwhelmed by several unknown words, or by other classmates being present. I've had students talk a lot, and read freely, when they arrived early, and there were just three or so of them. However, when other students started coming, they would clam up.

18. Allow them have a "reading buddy" like a stuffed animal, another favorite toy, etc. My daughter used to talk and sing to and "teach" her stuffed animals, and would sometimes "talk" through them to me. That may be a key for your otherwise-shy reader, to get the focus off themselves, so they'll relax and read out loud. Before COVID, some of the teachers in public schools I worked in let their younger elementary kids bring stuffed animals to class to read to aloud. They loved it!

19. Give them lots of praise and encouragement along the way. We all want to feel like we're doing a great job! Be selective, but pour it on as appropriate.

20. If you are a Believer in Jesus Christ and have the freedom, use Bible stories, worship song lyrics, and more for them to read.

About 7 years ago, I had my 5th graders (online) read out loud about our God-ordained country of the United States America and our flag (I learned from KLOVE.com that morning that it was Flag Day! God's timing is impeccable! So I seized this opportunity to brag on how God inspired people to found this country so we'd have the freedom to worship Him and love and live and promote His Word!).

I also had them read a pamphlet from a ministry which I scanned in, called "Student Legal Rights on Public School Campuses" (There were 10 listed, from RevivalFires.com).

After that, I had the students read out loud something I wrote years ago, called "The Great Plan." It is based on Jeremiah 29:11, although I didn't list the verse, but the heart of it, about the importance of choices and how they shape each student's life—and the lives of those around him or her. I wrote it to use as a discipline writing assignment—but the students loved it, and wanted extra copies to share! Hallelujah!

(Many people have become born again by learning English through reading God-breathed materials, so ask the LORD for wisdom and boldness, and to help you choose materials, then go for it!)

Of all these years of teaching in public schools, and online, I don't ever remember being challenged by a student, or a parent, and only once by administration (but not about having the kids read aloud).

The enemy attack (even though rather subtle, but easily perceived by me, with the help of the Holy Spirit, Who is Truth, and leads us into all truth) had to do with me writing, "Jesus loves you and so do I!" on the blackboard, and I was told to take it off, because "...we'd have to put (the names of others) on the board, too," etc. etc., *ad nauseum*.

Anyway, I said nothing, but the kids noticed Jesus's name was gone, and they were upset! I had told the principal who insisted I take it off respectfully but clearly, that "Jesus is the only One Who rose again, and that He's coming back, and that things are changing!" He didn't say anything, and the LORD told me to put, "You are loved by Everyone (Capital "Everyone"!) that matters!"

Go for it. The LORD your God will guide you, and He's always got your back!

But no weapon that is formed against you shall prosper, and every tongue that shall rise against you in judgment you shall show to be in the wrong. This [peace, righteousness, security, triumph over opposition] is the heritage of the servants of the Lord [those in whom the ideal Servant of the Lord is reproduced]; this is the righteousness or the vindication which they obtain from Me [this is that which I impart to them as their justification], says the Lord.—Isaiah 54:17, AMPC

Let Your Students Teach

And you shall teach them to your children, speaking of them when you sit in your house and when you walk along the road, when you lie down and when you rise up.—Deut. 11:19, AMPC

Every day that I teach, I say (as the Holy Spirit Who is God has taught me), "Master, You are the Teacher. You created these students and know what they need. I yield to You."

The LORD is so faithful! He has given me more students (whom I teach virtually) than ever this fall. Hallelujah! So I have asked Him for strategies to help each student with his or her unique needs.

He never fails to supply, and one strategy he gave me was to have my 7th grade student "teach" me, which empowered him—and caused him to have deeper insight on the math problem, as he explained every step of how to solve it. I have done this with younger students as well.

(I know many teachers have used this, but the LORD reminded me about it, and I believe this will be very effective as time goes on, for this student who's sometimes had challenges focusing on the material in front of him.)

This student was a little annoyed at first about it, but I counseled him and told him that, just like a coach invests more time and energy in the "most promising players" on the team, I'm giving him rigorous instruction, because I know he is a leader.

He appreciated that, although he still wasn't too interested in doing all the extra work of having to slow down and think about and explain every step.

He did well, though. I knew he was tired from a full week's worth of school, including running a few miles a day for a track team of which he was part.

So I had him pretend to be the teacher, and have me be the student. He was a little uncomfortable with that, but I told him that "in teaching, we learn," and that we have to truly understand each step of a process in order to explain it well.

We will continue this reiteration of what he has learned, and although it may not be extremely soon, I know he will appreciate this higher level of instruction. His mother does, and she is working closely with me for his success.

How much more does the Holy Spirit work with each of us, not only for our personal success, but for the benefit of others, and in very specific ways. He is so very good and faithful! We bless His name forever!

(As I reread this article from years before, I remembered that the LORD showed me to do this over 15 years ago, when my (then) 5th grade daughter came home, excited that she had learned to play the flute-like recorder.

I said something like, "Wow! Why don't you teach me? I've never learned to play one of those!"

I was delighted and a bit amazed that, at my request, her demeanor changed; this "grown-uppy" attitude and look came over her countenance! Her voice even had more authority, when she opened her mouth again, and I listened to her teach me—enraptured as much as her new "persona" as with the teaching techniques that she so eloquently shared.

The LORD may have been revealing to me that teaching/training is one of her spiritual gifts.

Indeed, she is a very responsible and creative leader in many ways, although not (yet) in an overtly "teaching" position. However, she has had her own graphics design business for a while, and is doing well!)

13 Ways to Empower Your Students

Power. From the time we are born, we all want it! Truly, we are born for it, but we are meant to use it to help others, to the glory of God.

Power is influence, and the world gets it by money, by beauty (although their standards are quite different than the LORD's, Who is THE most beautiful of all!), by humor, and other means.

Power from the LORD has quite a different Source and application.

7 For God has not given us a spirit of fear, but of power, love, and self-control. -2 Timothy 1:7, Berean Study Bible

The LORD Jesus Christ, Who is Love, empowers us by His Spirit of Grace, by His Sprit of Love.

God is Love, and all love comes from Him. Hallelujah!

7 Beloved, let us love one another, because love comes from God. Everyone who loves has been born of God and knows God. 8 Whoever does not love does not know God, because <u>God is love</u>. 9 This is how God's love was revealed among us: God sent His one and only Son into the world, so that we might live through Him. - I John 4:7-9, Berean Standard Bible (underline mine)

So how do we empower others? The same way we are empowered: by Love.

16And we know (understand, recognize, are conscious of, by observation and by experience) and believe (adhere to and put faith in and rely on) the love God cherishes for us. <u>God is love</u>, and he who dwells *and* continues in love dwells *and* continues in God, and God dwells *and* continues in him. – I John 4:16, AMPC (underline mine)

We are meant to soak up Love, and to give Love. Many students don't receive the Love they need at home, for various reasons; the main one, I believe, being because their parents don't fully understand the

Love of God for them. Indeed, it is truly an inexhaustible subject, but whatever loving actions and words we show our students can only make a positive impact—whether we ever mention the name of God of not.

This doesn't mean we are blatantly preaching about Jesus nor teaching the Word of God—nor are we avoiding the subject.

God has done so very much for me through the decades, and I'm really bold about my faith in Christ. In all my years of being in public schools and community organizations, it was a very rare occasion when a student didn't show joy at my witness (i.e., from mentioning "in passing" that God has given us a beautiful day, good sleep, fun things in school, etc. etc., or more specific boldness as the Holy Spirit led).

As educators, we have great influence, and it is an honor to be able to shape the lives of others, especially children.

The Great Teacher, the LORD Jesus Christ Who is Love, knows every student uniquely, for He created us all (Genesis 1:26-28)! We can ask Him to give us insight into each student and then yield to His Holy Spirit.

We ask Him to empower us to empower them. He always does! He is faithful, faithful, forever!

So, whether you are teaching in a school building; in a community center or daycare; at home; or online; here are some of the ways He helps us empower our students:

(1) Ask Him to fill you afresh with Himself every morning, and to make you sensitive and obedient to His Spirit; to let His gentleness (and all the fruit of the Spirit—Galatians 5:22!) rise up in you. Also, asking Him to put His Words in your mouth is something powerful that He will do for us.

(2) See each student as unique, and as a gift from Him. He trusts us to teach these students, and it is not an accident that they are in our lives, for Him to work through us to impart love and wisdom and educational strategies to them.

(3) Be affectionate towards them. I am that way, and I've not yet met a student (even an adult, really) who didn't like it when I call them "Sweetheart," "Precious," "Darling," and such—all as terms of endearment to the glory of God.

(I had one older elementary male student question why I was calling him that, but I explained to him in front of the class that it was just something that flowed out of me, and he started receiving it. I pray it was the beginning of healing for his heart, for it seemed he came from a rough and most likely unloving background.)

(4) Use humor and encouragement as appropriate. Look for things to praise in each student, but not overdoing it. As the LORD told one well-known pastor, "You need to laugh more!" Indeed, the Word says, in Proverbs 15:13, **"A joyful heart makes a cheerful face..."** (NASB)

Also, Proverbs 12:25 says, **"Anxiety weighs down the heart of a man, but a good word cheers it up."**

(5) Let the students be more active. These kiddos are raised on technology, and they like it. They are also usually very good with it, from typing to drawing with the interactive markers on the electronic whiteboards, etc.

They will usually be more engaged if they are doing something with their hands. I'm glad that, over the past 30 years, education has moved more to a student-centric style of teaching.

Almost all students need us to guide them, especially elementary age, but when we allow them to do instead of just listen and watch, they learn much more. This works for all learners, not just those labeled "kinesthetic."

(6) Let them bring things to show you—whether it's photos of their families, or art they created, or a story they wrote; recounts of sports games, or singing a short song or even playing an instrument in your class; as there is time, of course.

We have "show and tell" ever so often. I have found that students of every elementary age love this, and giving up a few minutes of instruction time every couple of weeks or so is a good investment in strong relationships, and not a waste of time.

Once, I had an athletically-inclined online student carry his laptop outside and do a forward flip on his big trampoline (with his mom close by, as I was going, "Be safe! Be safe!"). Show and tell keeps things interesting—for the kids, the parents, and the teacher!

(7) Share personal things from your life too. I have shown some students my family pics, art drawn by my talented mother and daughter, stories and poems I've written, and props I have (stuffed animals, paintings I've done, even though I'm definitely an amateur (but just being confident enough to share my efforts with them is inspiring to them).

(8) Let them "teach" you. One form of reiteration or "retelling" that the LORD showed me, in order to assess that the student has truly comprehended or understood the lesson, is to ask them to "teach" me, or explain back to me—through telling or demonstration—what I just taught them.

This has worked well for me with almost every student, no matter how young, except perhaps during the first couple of sessions, where we are still getting to know each other.

This is especially effective if there is an interactive whiteboard, at the front of a public school class, or on an interactive whiteboard. I've even seen some students gain confidence almost instantly, as they realize they are now in the "teacher" role, however temporary! It's an amazing confidence boost!

(9) Be gentle in correction, whether academically or emotionally. Affirm the positives, and address the negatives by reminding the student(s) of expectations and how we all need to follow them to help each other have a good time and learn as much as possible.

(10) Share expectations at the beginning of the relationship. From my experience teaching many years in public schools, and now for

many months online, this is usually not needed teaching one-on-one/ private classes online.

Most students getting private tutoring—especially elementary—have an adult right next to them, listening to and watching the whole session, or at least in the room where they can hear what's going on.

Sometimes, kids get really excited and want to use the tools on the interactive white board. It can be fine for them to draw while they listen—as long as you perceive that they are truly listening and not being distracted. You can assess this orally, by asking them questions as you're teaching.

My daughter (who is now a professional artist, with a university degree in art), used to draw in church, and otherwise, and the LORD helped me understand she was still learning while she did that. He revealed to me that I'm the same way—only I take notes; do a lot of writing.

The point it, the hand is in motion, whether it's writing or art, and for some of us, that helps us be more engaged in the material we are learning.) So ask the LORD for wisdom about each student!

(11) Always commend them for telling the truth, which usually means they say, "I don't know." There have been sometimes when a student said that just being unengaged or bored, but usually, they just haven't heard the concept or word I'm teaching.

I often have stated that I am learning things too, and some students have actually taught me things—either cool facts about something we're discussing, or technological things that help my teaching be more efficient! I am sure to thank and brag on them about that. We all like to help each other!

(12) Let peers help each other. Some of my classes have 9 students, and I see all their precious faces at once. They can all hear me, and the student who's speaking at the time.

If I ask one student to read a text and he or she struggles with a word, I've taught them to say, "I need some help with this word."

Then either I ask who wants to help, or the other students will raise their hands if they want to help, without me prompting them. (They're getting better at doing it without me asking.)

I let the student needing help choose whom he or she wants to help. If the answer is not quite correct, I gently praise them for being willing to help, and praise whatever part was right, then tell them the correct answer.

This is an excellent way for all the students not only to hear the mistakes and the right answers, but to understand more about how to gently correct each other.

I also allow the students to comment on one another's work—it has to be constructive, of course. I have found that doing these things builds community among my students, and strengthens their understanding that I believe in them.

(13) Remember to pray for God's will to be done in each student's life and family, and to release any and all worries or concerns about your students and their families to the LORD. Initially, they are His kids and He is working in their lives—through you and others—and He is responsible for them.

I know we love our sweet students, and they become "our kids"—even the adults, or at least sometimes—because the LORD Who is the loving Father of all wants the best for every person.

We are His Ambassadors (2 Cor. 5:20).

Yet, He does not want us to be burdened down by worry about them. So we can ask for His grace to let Him work through us, answer our prayers, and release them to Him as we trust Him to do what's best for them.

After all, as He revealed to me years ago, we trust Him totally—with ourselves and everything else!—when we go to sleep at night. If we didn't trust Him, we'd never sleep!

(As He told me once, "While you're sleeping, I am keeping you..." Yes, the Great I AM is watching over us—and those we love! Hallelujah!!)

These tips can help empower your students, and the LORD will be faithful to give you even more strategies as you implement these, and ask Him for more!

Remember, you are not the teacher; *Jesus the Christ is*. Yield to Him, and He will "put His super on your natural", for He is with you and for you, forever!

Nathanael answered, Rabbi (Teacher), You are the Son of God; You are the King of Israel.—John 1:49, Amplified Bible

Reading Buddies Can Help

Train up a child in the way he should go [and in keeping with his individual gift or bent], and when he is old he will not depart from it.—Proverbs 22:6, AMPC

Are you having challenges getting your child(ren) to read? Let them use a "reading buddy"—a stuffed animal or a toy. This will encourage them to read out loud, and explain as they go, and even use more vocal variety to make it more interesting for their "buddy."

These "buddies" can be amazing emotional and mental support for your student(s), to encourage them to read more and more, and to know that someone is "listening".

As we teachers know, the better a student can read, the more they are helped in being able to understand every subject.

As I discovered when teaching math in public school, there can be quite a bit of reading even in that subject, especially in the "dreaded" reading problems.

(I used to hate those myself. After all, who really cares whether Jimmy left Abilene on the train at 3 a.m., and arrived in time to be able to eat his Aunt Drenda's apple pie while it was hot? ☺ I didn't, anyway, and I was a good reader. But a big part of helping kids learn to read well is to help them learn to also use context clues, and separate facts from one another, so they are not confused (like I was), and can gain true understanding of how to solve the problem. As I've exhorted many math students, learning how to solve such problems will help them learn to solve problems in life too. I'm not sure they all believed me, but I still preached it!)

When our students learn the skills of reading—not just pronouncing the words well, but being truly fluent, they are good readers, it helps them in every subject.

So, if they can not only read out loud to their "buddies" (whether another student or the toy/animal), and then, even better, explain the concepts behind what they are reading, then their understanding is strengthened and increased.

As Roman philosopher Lucius Annaeus Seneca the Younger is quoted, "By teaching we learn."

Even better, as Timothy writes in the Word of God: **And the [instructions] which you have heard from me along with many witnesses, transmit *and* entrust [as a deposit] to reliable *and* faithful men who will be competent *and* qualified to teach others also.** - 2 Timothy 2:2, AMPC

The kids are leaders *now!*

Children love stuffed animals. Unless there are restrictions against it because of covid or other mess, letting your child(ren) have a "reading buddy" such as a stuffed animal or toy is a great way to excite them about reading!

I've seen this used in public schools, and it works well. The children are excited to bring a favorite toy or animal from home (This was before the pandemic. I'm not sure what the rules are now, but if the kids have to wear a mask anyway, I don't see why they couldn't bring their buddies!), and look forward to the official time they get to read to their buddy.

Also, I liked to keep disinfectant spray and wipes handy in the classrooms, and you can require the student to have their inanimate "buddy" cleaned before using it in the classroom.

So encouraging your students to utilize reading buddies is a great way to keep the kids positively productive, while the busy teacher (or parent) gets a few moments to do something else.

(In addition, you can charge your more responsible students with "monitoring" the younger ones, to make sure that what is being spoken doesn't break any classroom rules. You can let the kids swap out these leadership roles, as well. ☺)

This works at home as well as at school. The child will hear his or her own voice reading the text (You can use this strategy for any subject, including math!), and thus hearing the facts, so this is a win-win: they are receiving the information through their eyes and ears, simultaneously, while also doing a "good deed" to "help" their buddy.

This works with live pets, too, at home. (Also, there was a live (service) dog that would visit the local public library for the kids to read to.)

When I was homeschooling my daughter in her 6th and 7th grades, she would often share information she learned—such as the solar system, and the various denominations of money, etc.—with her Siamese Fighting Fish, who was in the bowl on the bookshelf behind her. Prince never protested, but seemed attentive. (It could have been a ploy to make sure he didn't miss a meal, but we're not sure. Anyway, he was a great listener! This helped her enjoy speaking the information, which was being put into her memory in a more satisfying way than just reading it silently.)

Several studies have proven that, when we experience something exciting, that moment and/or information can be "burned into our brains." That is why it is super-important that we allow only the good experiences, as much as possible!

These techniques won't hurt your child(ren); they can help greatly in the enjoyment, fluency, confidence, and recall of your student. So let your child(ren) pick a reading buddy today, and get going!

Teaching With Think-Alouds

This is information I learned about "think-alouds," to teach reading to elementary students:

A "think-aloud" is where a teacher reads a text aloud and asks herself questions or otherwise comments as she reads, to model for the students the strategies to use to comprehend what they need to gain from the text(s); appropriate ways they should think aloud to self-assess and increase comprehension as they make predictions, ask themselves questions, find answers, make connections to real world issues and experiences, and consider many details when figuring out what they need to know about the text(s) they are reading.

During a student think-aloud, students are coached by the teacher as they go along, but they also think aloud—speak their thoughts—about what strategies to use to figure out what the text means and what they should gain from it.

Questions are needed in a think-aloud, for the teacher to guide the student with specific questions through the text and the student's correct interpretation and comprehension of it, as the student searches for and finds the answers. The questions also prompt the student to stay on track, stay engaged, and look for the answers truly needed to comprehend the text as fully as possible.

Think-alouds can be used to assess students, because they provide an explicit understanding of the student's thoughts about the texts. If the teacher needs to correct something, the teacher can immediately address the issue as she hears the student speaking.

If a student doesn't understand something in a text, they can use strategies such as context clues or a dictionary to discover the meaning of unknown words; to reread the text and connect to previous experience or real-world issues; to look at other clues in the text to see settings and character actions and other things that may provide consistency and show whether the student's thoughts about the thing confusing him may or may not flow with the text; to summarize out loud or in his mind what he already knows about the text; to allow the teacher to ask more questions to help guide him the right way.

Students can make predictions before reading, then as the student learns information while reading, he may modify the prediction to better fit the story. After reading, he may use them to connect to real-world knowledge, verify the theme, and summarize the work.

Here are my definitions of terms applicable to think-alouds:

Dialogic Reading - Students tell or read a story, while the teacher listens. The teacher has the student(s) (alone or in small groups) read the story at least once, asking questions to help guide them to deeper understanding.

CROWD - Completion; Recall; Open Ended questions and statements; the 5 W's (Who/What/Why/When/Where?); and connections to real-world experiences

PEER - Prompt; Evaluate ; Expand; and Repeat.

Tripod Response Sheet - Personal (journaling), Creative (Reader's Theater or other acting out of the text), and Critical (opinion essay).

Think-Pair-Share - Students are assigned a buddy or small group and asked to predict, think of questions, decide on theme, etc.) They talk with the buddy or small group first, then share with the entire class.

These ideas can help you understand your reading students and teach them more effectively.

Act It Out: Reader's Theater And More

Writers want their readers to have an excellent vicarious experience from their work. One way to infuse your writing with realistic effects, especially in fiction, is to act out what your characters are thinking, speaking, and doing.

This can involve facial expressions, other body language, and even volume and tone of voice as you speak out loud what your characters are or will or might say.

You are truly "becoming" your character(s), and acting out their lives.

Your students will really enjoy doing this, whether they're reading out of a book, from printed pages for "reader's theatre," or acting out a poem or song or article they wrote themselves. This will be kinesthetic engagement, and it's fun for almost all humans, no matter what the age.

To do this effectively, we must know our characters, and how they would respond in certain situations—even during trauma or very unusual circumstances.

So another tip is to have your students (1) read about the characters (more reading practice! Yay!); (2) discuss the characters with a buddy or in a small group; (3) write out character descriptions for each character, making them unique from one another so there is no confusion in your mind, nor the reader's. Then (4) have them act out how they think the character would respond, according to the text(s), or even in a make-believe situation, before practicing the actual assignment.

(You can do many assessments during all of this!)

You can use examples of how "real writers" understand their characters: For instance, my main character, Princess Pearl, has been raised in a loving, stable Christian home since she was created by God in her mother's womb. But she meets a young teen that has had the opposite life, and the teen cannot usually understand where Pearl is coming from.

I created these characters a few years ago, and know them well. So when Pearl starts talking about God, and looking up a verse in Exodus, Xi—who has never read the Bible—can only think of Exodus as a great name for a rock group. As Pearl is telling Xi about Genesis 50:20, where the LORD works all the junk of the enemy for good, Xi wonders about that, because of her very rough life, and an extremely traumatic experience with her mom—and no dad in the picture.

However, as Christian writers, above all, we must know the character of God, and convey this to our readers as much as possible—no matter what's going on in our characters' lives. That is our mission as writers for Him on this planet.

So it is very important that, while Pearl (who is younger than Xi) is doing all she knows to be the best witness to Xi and share the truth with her, she also be open to correction by her loving mother and other believing adults, and most of all, to the Spirit of God living in her heart.

The main thing, of course, is to ask the LORD—Elohim, the Creator and Author of all good things—to write through you, and guide your mind and hands, so that what He wants flows through you. He knows exactly what your readers need and want to read, to be drawn closer to Him.

I've been amazed sometimes at some scenes He's written through me. Some have been emotional experiences for me as He's writing them—including while acting them out—and I've had to ask Him to make sure it was Him, and not just my emotions or memories or other soulish things!

God is a faithful Father, and the Prince of Peace. His Holy Spirit is the Spirit of Truth Who leads us in right paths, always, and John 16:13 (AMPC) states: But when he, the Spirit of truth, comes, he will guide you into all the truth. He will not speak on his own; he will speak only what he hears, and he will tell you what is yet to come.

So if you write something and it just doesn't seem to fit in your current work, keep it and ask the LORD where else it may fit; possibly it is an article on its own.

You can also involve your students even more. Ask them their opinions. *How would they add to this selection, or otherwise modify it? Might they combine it with another story they already know, just to think differently for a bit, to spark more creative ideas? What do they like best, and think should be left out, if anything?* And so on.

God is faithful, and He will help you to help you and your students to "act it out"!

All Your commandments are faithful and sure.... Psalm 119:86a, AMPC

JESUS IS LORD!

Tips for Teaching Online

The words of the reckless pierce like swords, but the tongue of the wise brings healing. - Proverbs 12:18, NIV

For over 40 years, I've been teaching many students many things. For over half a year, I've been teaching online. Here are tips and strategies I've learned that I believe will help you be more prepared and successful in teaching online if you choose to!

Teaching a small group has different dynamics than teaching one student. That should be apparent, but after teaching one-on-one online for months, tutoring elementary students in various subjects, I had to adjust to a cross between teaching one at a time and past experiences of teaching 20-something students in a public brick-and-mortar school.

Eight (even four) students can feel like many more, if you're not prepared to accommodate different learning styles and personalities (This is what public schools call "Differentiated Instruction." You are expected to modify your manner and instruction to help every kind of student you could possibly have.

This can seem impossible, but the LORD gives us wisdom, grace, and divine strategies for success, praise Him!). God our Father is always with us. He knows our hearts to help these precious kiddos, and He alone is the Source of all we need to succeed in teaching (or any other field!).

There are many forms of online teaching, and I have experienced several. There are group teaching experiences, such as the group of 49 students (in one class!) in a major city in China, whom I taught online. Having their main teacher in the room was a definite help, as was learning to say the students' names in Chinese, so that I could personally call on them. However, I spoke English otherwise, because it was English class.

(By the way, Chinese kids are just like kids from any other nation. They can be noisy, especially as they come in; they like jokes and often giggle from nervousness or for other reasons; they may clam up and not respond, although usually, the Chinese children are taught to respect teachers and obey quickly. They are expected to have high standards, and fulfilling the requirements for teaching group classes can be stringent.)

For these, you need to learn how to properly say their names in their language, and keep accurate records, while doing multiple things at once. For instance, in this class, I was required to address as many students as possible by name each class, and make a tic mark on the roll by their names to prove that I had done so. That was a bit overwhelming, trying to remember how to say their names, recognize them in the big class—where it was hard to see their faces—plus teach, and then remember upon whom I'd called.

I was not able to complete the entire semester with these students because of challenges with internet connections. It was clear to me that the problem was not on my end, and the Chinese tech (who was not very patient) kept telling me to try the same thing to correct the problem, and promised to set up a time to address the specific issue—but never did.

I appealed to the director (who happened to be British, and with whom I had a good relationship), but nothing was done, either for the internet connection, nor for the app I was supposed to install on my cell phone—that never worked because of blocks by the US government, and, I believe, by the Chinese government as well.

Because of the internet challenges, my class was given to a sub, and I did not appreciate that. I resigned. Then, my reputation/name was "dinged" on an internet site that many Chinese companies refer to when checking on applicants.

I was a little frustrated, but I know the LORD always has my back. With all of the negative vibes between the USA and China, I wished them well and was glad the portal was closed between me and them.

Since then, the LORD has opened many more wonderful doors that I would never have found, if I'd stayed teaching kids in China! I'm not knocking it, if that's what God has for anyone. It was just not the right path for me!

Still, I picked up a few tips and strategies that I've used in other forms of teaching, so I consider it education.

So teaching online can be one-on-one (often written as 1:1); one-to-many (1:49, such as my class in China); or small groups of 4-8, or perhaps more.

(At the time of this writing;2020) I currently teach students I teach from a public school in another state which is really locked down by the virus. The kids, bless their hearts, are totally confined to their homes. (We pray that will change soon, so they can go back to being with each other at school in person, even wearing masks and standing six feet apart!)

In my online class, they can see each other, and some of them know each other from going to the brick and mortar school.

It's great that they are relaxed—until they decided suddenly to turn off the camera; talk to their older brother—who seems to not care that they are supposed to be learning; go get a live puppy or cat to play with; pick up a purple balloon and blow it up so big I can't see their faces; carry the computer to another room; turn on their mikes so I can hear all the background noise; or, even worse, figure out how to turn off my mike, so that my voice and the class are interrupted (This has happened more than once in Google Hangouts, the platform I'm required to use, and I don't like it at all.)!

However the kids with whom I've had these challenges, labeled "struggling learners" by their school (and the only reason some of them are labeled that way is, I think, because they are not behind but just have had challenges staying engaged, because they are so used to multi-media video games and TV shows, etc. And these kids are only in first, second, and third grades!), still have that innocent sweetness that little ones do. They truly want to please the teacher and earn rewards, and be commended for good work.

I do love 'em and they know that. The first day, some of them asked me to send them some books. I told them that I have truly written and published many books, and that I'd be happy to do so—if they approve it with their parents and the company for whom I work. The kids were excited, but none of the parents mentioned it, so they probably forgot to ask.

For integrity's sake, I mentioned their request to the director and told her I'd be happy to send books, because I sow them all over the world, as the LORD directs, mentioning that I'd told the kids to check with their parents. I made it plain that I write Christian and inspirational books. While I don't think the director or the parents would mind the kids getting free books (at my expense, and especially positive ones like I write!), the anti-Christ spirit that's bound the education system doesn't like things like that.

However, as I told one public school principal, who told me that I had to erase "Jesus loves you and so do I," from my fourth grade whiteboard, "because," as he stated, "if you don't, then we'd have to put Mohammed's and Buddha's and other names up there."

As I told my fourth graders later—when they asked why I'd erased that part (and were indignant, bless their precious hearts!)—I just looked at him calmly, and said, "You know He is the only One that rose from the dead!" and then, "Things are changing!"

He left without comment. I didn't like it, but I wanted to be obedient. The principal was probably having to enforce the "school" rules. So I asked the LORD what to put, and He quickly helped me understand to replace what had been there with, "You are loved by Every One that matters!" The principal found some excuse to zip up minutes after he'd commanded me to change the wording, and saw my new expression. Now how could he argue with the wisdom of God?

To be fair, the same school later allowed the Gideons to come and allow the fifth graders to choose a Bible if they wanted—on school time, on school grounds, at a break time. Praise God!

So, being able to teach online allows more freedom to sow the Word, in my opinion! I'm teaching from my house, and I can choose what I want in my background!

I have a saying the LORD gave me years ago, that I painted and display prominently where every student can see it—those across the world, those in public school, and everyone in between. It states: *"Invest. Connect. Empower. LOVE. Aren't you glad God did?! John 3:16"*.

Freedom is a wonderful thing!

There are many similarities to teaching school in a building. For instance, remembering to recognize and call on every student throughout the lesson, while also remembering to adjust speaking speeds, expectations, and more (especially due to the fact that, while most of these lower elementary kiddos were bilingual, a couple were native Spanish ELLs), caused me to flex in new ways.

Part of this was adjusting to the new curriculum, which was straightforward enough, but which was a struggle at the beginning of the semester, because the delivery of my manuals was delayed a week due to an ice storm. Having been raised "old school," I was not as comfortable or adept at using electronic versions of the books. Added to that the fact that mine were an older version (with somewhat different wording!) made for an awkward 10 days or so, till I received my books.)

Then there was the bathroom thing. This is only a 50-minute class, yet I still have had kids interrupt the class to go to the bathroom! After a few days of this, I finally remembered to ask the students to be sure to go to the bathroom before class started. Having been used to teaching mostly upper elementary in public school, I had to remind myself that these younger kiddos didn't have as solid a concept of time as the older ones did.

In addition, these kids were all in their homes. This helped them be more comfortable in some ways, I suppose, but also created distractions. I had one older brother picking at one student, so that, as I was teaching, I saw my student laughing, looking off, and not at all paying attention—which required me to interrupt the class to politely demand that he focus and stop talking to anyone outside of our class.

Other times, the kids would suddenly pick up their laptops and carry them to another room. After being distracted by this a few times, I finally understood they were truly trying to find a place where they could focus better. I realized this more as I'd have the kids occasionally turn on their audio to repeat the Affirmation (more on that in a moment).

Some would just turn off their cameras and then I'd have to say, "Please keep your video on, so I can see your handsome/beautiful face!" Some would raise their hand and ask. It was still an interruption to the teaching.

To be fair, these are lower elementary students, and some still even had a lisp (sweet little first and second graders!).

Yet, they are also savvy in many ways—especially in technology. One of the first days, my audio kept going off, and it was a terrible interruption. I would start to teach, and the audio would stop, and the kids would go, "We can't hear you!" I was patiently trying all the things I knew—then I got a message on the screen from the tech, that a certain student was turning off my audio! I was slightly shocked; I didn't know the students had that power! (This was in a certain well-known meeting room of a well-known search engine, and I hope they change that—very soon!)

I didn't waste any time, but addressed the student directly, in front of the class. After all, he'd interrupted my class—several times, and the wrong should be exposed. I was not rude, but firm.

The next day, he did it again, but I busted him, again, in front of the class. This time I left a comment on his electronic file, and also reported him to my director.

In addition, one morose-looking male student, whom I'd been patient with, waiting for him to start obeying and showing me his work on his white board (or paper), finally barked at me, "I typed them in the chat!"

OK, this is new too—I had no idea the students would use the chat for their answers! "That's great, (student), I said, but we are not using the chat in this class." At that, he looked even more bored. "However," I continued, hoping to encourage him, "we might use it later on for polls or something." It might have been all right, but most of these very young students didn't type, or didn't type fast enough, to make it efficient for the whole class.

"We are all going to write in this class," I told them. "It's good to type, but it has been proven that you can actually remember things better if you write them."

When I finally got my books days later, it was a great relief! I was able to see and touch what I'd been teaching, and I was more settled and organized. The LORD also reminded me to tell the class they could write in their books. I would write in mine as we went through lessons—both for examples for them (and especially for my English Language Learners, as I communicated with them in my basic Spanish speech, while making a mental note to expand my Spanish!), and also to make notes as I taught.

I encouraged them to write, both in their books, and on their white boards or paper. While reminding them to stay focused on the tasks, I also reminded them they could write or draw other things about the lessons to help them remember. I shared with them that I liked to take notes, even at church (That was a subtle plug for God; I sow such seeds wherever I can!) and while reading books, and that my daughter often drew pictures at school and church while she was listening.

This prompted me to redo my expectations, and to add a couple, i.e., "Please do not touch your computer, except for audio." I had made a list of expectations that I reviewed at the beginning of class every day.

However, the LORD prompted me to be more positive. Instead of "Do not..." He showed me how to flip it. I made a new list of expectations, on a brightly-colored poster, that started looked like this:

YOU CAN DO THESE!

1.Stand up while you listen and work

2.Write and draw (on your paper or whiteboards and books)

3.Raise your hand when you have a question or comment

4.Help others

5.Earn rewards and have fun

6.Keep your hands off your computer except for audio

7.Learn lots every day

With the help of God, you can implement these tips and strategies to become a more effective educator. Go for it, and may the LORD give you abundant joy and satisfaction as you serve as a catalyst for positive change in the lives of your students!

Strategies and Satisfactions: Teaching ELLs

The LORD says in Matthew 28:18-20 and other places to **"go and teach all nations..."**

He is, of course, talking about teaching them His ways, His Word. That is why we Believers in Jesus Christ are on the planet.

However, the Holy Spirit has to work and prepare the hearts of those to whom we minister, to get them ready to acknowledge that they need help; they need Christ.

Meanwhile, He calls us to "be ready in season and out of season" and to walk in Love toward others. We are Christ's Ambassadors, because He is making His appeal through us!

One of the main ways we show the love of Christ—that we show that Jesus is real and alive and cares for His creation of people—is by helping others.

Teaching English to non-native speakers—English Language Learners (ELLs) is one fun and meaningful way to do that. While many people do it free, as a ministry, there are numerous companies in the USA and overseas who are eager to hire native speakers of English.

(So you can, with a little training, use the gift of speaking what you've known for years to help others come to Christ! (More on that in a moment!))

It is a major blessing to be a native speaker of English, which is considered by almost all populations to the be the #1 universal language, and people from diverse cultures are eager to learn English, for education, for business, for travel, and more.

It helps if you already have teaching experience, and especially if you have a TEFL (Teacher of English as a Foreign Language) or TESOL (Teacher of English as a Second or Other Language) certification, but you can now get a certification in this for much less money and time than even just a few years ago. Many companies that hire English teachers also have the training for you to earn a TEFL/TESOL.

China is the country that hires the most teachers, at present, although there are many countries who hire English teachers. You don't have to know Chinese, nor use it. They want you to speak entirely in English, for submersion for the students.

There are many countries and companies that hire native English speakers, and some even hire teachers or tutors that are fluent in English, even though it is a second or third language.

Some companies hire for simple conversation, while others can go much more in depth, with complex speaking and writing of English.

My experience in teaching English to speakers of other languages has proved to me that almost every student I've encountered, whether child or adult, is very respectful and appreciative of the teacher.

Although some of the students may know several languages (for the USA is about the only advanced country where students often only know one language—English!), they see English as a very powerful tool to help them have a better life.

A better life is what God wants for us all. So, by helping others to learn English, and by being encouraging, patient, positive, and attuned to the unique needs and desires of each student, we are showing the love of Christ. Besides, as I tell Him before each session, He is the Master Teacher, Who created each student and knows them intimately.

He knows exactly what they need, and I trust Him to guide me to the right materials, preparation, and execution during each session. He is always faithful to do so, and it is such a joy to yield to Him and let His Spirit flow through me!

Although not every student is a perfect fit, they see my earnest desire to help, and appreciate it. Sometimes, a student needs a different teacher, but almost all of my students enjoy and learn and give good reviews. They and their parents are very pleased with my God-anointed efforts.

By preparing with excellence, and showing other loving, gentle, patient, and cheerful ways, I am demonstrating Christ to them. Also, as He flows through me, I am blessed; highly satisfied and amazed that I get paid to do something that brings such deep rewards!

In addition, since I have freedom on the platforms on which I teach to utilize my own methods and decorate my own backdrop and classroom wall, I have a few Christian symbols. I may not talk about them directly.

On occasion, though, I have been thrilled when a student asks what I think about God, or mentions prayer, or something. That is an open door to plant more seeds for the LORD, in a few words or sentences, and then get back to the instruction of English.

One example is when I had a darling second grader from Africa, who was in America at the time of our lesson. During our first lesson—which I'd done for the past five years, with almost every one of my online students in public schools and homes, across the USA and in 8 other countries—I told her I pray every day for God to help me help my students, and that I pray for all my past, present, and future students. (This is still true today, and the number of those I cover in my daily prayers grows often.)

Several lessons after we'd first met, she started asking questions about God, and I would answer generally, then redirect her to English. However, when the questions persisted (and some evidence about fear of flying, for she said she and her family were going within a few days to visit Africa), and I could tell she was not just trying to get out of the lesson (She was very intelligent, and "grown-uppy" from the beginning!), I started actively ministering the truth to her.

With the help of the Holy Spirit of Truth, I bragged on LORD Jesus, told her we all must have Him as Savior and LORD, and within a minute or two, she had received Christ! Hallelujah! So she is part of the proof that my prayers for "past, present, and future students" are working, because I'd been praying that way for at least a couple years before I met her, my future student! Hallelujah!

I was thrilled that, now, she had the LORD of Heaven and earth with her, and He would not only keep her safe, but comfort her, assuaging her fears and helping her to grow in trusting Him! Hallelujah!

Another tip for teaching non-native speakers of English is to guide the conversation; speak slowly enough so that they can understand you; ask often if they have any questions; make notes as you assess (test their understanding) of their progress; always show them proper respect; be gentle but firm if you have to redirect wrong behavior; have plenty of materials of various kinds to use; and to do what you say you will do for them.

Otherwise, a major part of teaching non-native speakers is to affirm their efforts, even the smallest ones. Most non-native speakers of English—even though the ones I've encountered are accomplished doctors, lawyers, education administrators, and other professionals—are speaking very understandable English, but have not been confident that they are speaking well.

So a big part of teaching English is to encourage the students, children and adults, and remind them that they are doing a good job!

Notice even the smallest steps they have accomplished, and if you need to, stop and celebrate by jumping up and down, giving them virtual 'high fives" while smiling broadly; clapping and doing other things that show your delight and pleasure in them work for both children and adults!

I also pray for all of my students and their families, of course, in my daily morning prayer time. In addition, if they share sad things with me, I show my compassion.

We often may have stupid stereotypes about people of other cultures; biases, judgments, based on wrong things we've heard from others. We must get rid of them, and remember that God is Jewish.

Jesus is a Jew! He is not American, nor any other race—yet all races come from Him, and He knows every language perfectly!

We must remember that, no matter where we were born, where we live, or what language(s) we speak, if we are born again by our faith in the shed blood and resurrection of Christ Jesus the LORD, then we are no longer citizens of earth, but of Heaven!

But there's far more to life for us. We're citizens of high heaven! We're waiting the arrival of the Savior, the Master, Jesus Christ, who will transform our earthy bodies into glorious bodies like his own. He'll make us beautiful and whole with the same powerful skill by which he is putting everything as it should be, under and around him.— Philippians 3:20,21, The Message

Thank the LORD He opened up the Covenant to all the rest of us! Let us remember that we are all part of the whole, and God the Father and Jesus the Son and the dear Holy Spirit (the Holy Trinity!) love each person ever born the same!

God is no Respecter of persons, nor should we be. We must respect people of other cultures, while never compromising our Biblical values and mandates.

Teaching English is an excellent way to visit other nations, while never getting on a plane! It's a wonderful way to discover fascinating details about how others live, and to share neat things about your own life.

Truly, teaching ESL (English as a Second Language) is a powerful tool for those to whom the LORD has given the desire and ability to do so. One way to teach ESL is to use the Bible and other Christian materials, while making it plain from the beginning that those are the main types of texts that will be used.

If that's you, go for it! God will help you, and He will draw all men unto Him as you lift Him up—whether you blatantly use the Bible, or not, for as the Word says, we are "living epistles"—letters from Christ that all men can read!

2 [No] you yourselves are our letter of recommendation (our credentials), written in your hearts, to be known (perceived, recognized) and read by everybody. 3 You show and make obvious that you are a letter from Christ delivered by us, not written with ink but with [the] Spirit of [the] living God, not on tablets of stone but on tablets of human hearts. —II Corinthians 3:2-3, AMPC

Accommodating Spanish ELLs

The wicked flee when no man pursues them, but the [uncompromisingly] righteous are bold as a lion.—Proverbs 28:1, AMPC

To me, Spanish is a beautiful language, practical to learn (especially with the influx of thousands more Spanish-speaking families into the USA!), and is one of the easiest languages to learn, because there are many similarities between Spanish and English.

Also, knowing the LORD leads us by desire and what we're good at, and still having been interested in learning Spanish after at least 10 years, I decided to pursue learning more, especially to help my students.

Although my primary goal in learning Spanish was to advance the Gospel, I'd finally settled it that the LORD had called me to the ministry of education, and being bilingual in Spanish is a very useful and practical tool.

The LORD has a wonderful way of opening up conversations where He can be glorified, and I'd noticed that, when I'd used words or short phrases in Spanish with my bilingual students in various educational settings, it always seemed to bless them.

So, I was drawn to this student who needed a Spanish-speaking tutor.

I'd been learning Spanish off and on for a few years, and decided to be bold and apply to help a fifth grade Spanish student—who spoke no English, really.

I knew enough to communicate pretty well, although I figured that, for this 20-question exam, with many paragraphs of text which would also have to be translated, I could depend on the better online sites to help me.

Mainly, though, I depended on God's Word and His faithfulness to be my ever-present Help.

Moment by moment, He is with us, knows exactly what we need, and supplies it, when we lean on Him!

But the Comforter (Counselor, Helper, Intercessor, Advocate, Strengthener, Standby), the Holy Spirit, Whom the Father will send in My name [in My place, to represent Me and act on My behalf], He will teach you all things. And He will cause you to recall (will remind you of, bring to your remembrance) everything I have told you.—John 14:26, AMPC

I decided that, with *El Senor Jesucristo*—He Who created every language and people group, Who knows *Español* perfectly; Who has promised to always be with me and help me—would help me succeed and give this precious student exactly what she needed.

I have strength for all things in Christ Who empowers me [I am ready for anything and equal to anything through Him Who infuses inner strength into me; I am self-sufficient in Christ's sufficiency].—Philippians 4:13, AMPC

Overall, the Spanish-speaking people are very warm, patient, and encouraging. They are big on God and family. They enjoy it when we English speakers learn their language.

(One thing to remember—which I wondered about until the LORD taught me—was that the children (and even some of the men, I've noticed) often are instructed to not look an adult in the eye, because it might be considered disrespect. So if the students don't look you in the eye, given them the benefit of the doubt, that they are working to be respectful. As long as they are following your instructions to the best of their abilities, then all should be well.)

So, getting back to my new student: Things went even better than I'd thought they would, (*Por supuesto*—of course!), and we were all delighted (her parents included)! The LORD gave me strategies to help this little one, and we are making good progress.

That's the way Dios—God—works. It's always a win-win with Him!

Ask Him to open opportunities for you, and give you peace about the ones (and the people) you should be connected with. He is our good, good Father, our faithful Shepherd, and loves to help us!

If you are wondering if you can speak Spanish and be understood, I say, *Si puedes hablar español y ser comprendida*! Yes, you can speak Spanish and be understood!

God is with you and for you. Go for it!

Helping My Spanish ELLs Online

I delight to do Your will, O my God; Your law is within my heart.
—Psalm 40:8, Berean Study Bible

As Psalm 37:4 says, when we delight ourselves in Him, He gives us the desires and secret petitions of our hearts.

As various Bible-based ministers have stated, this doesn't mean He gives us whatever we want. It means He works with us through His Spirit and His Word to align our desires with His, and then it is easy for Him to give us what we desire, for our desires are of Him, and thus we are delighted!

The LORD knows all things. God is good! (*¡Dios es bueno!*)

I have admired the Spanish language and desired to speak more of it through the years, knowing that, ultimately, the LORD Jesus Christ (*El Señor Jesucristo*) will use it as a tool to communicate with others to draw them to Himself.

Very recently, the LORD gave me a position as an online reading tutor for lower elementary kids, where there is a large Latino population. I was excited for many reasons—including the opportunity to truly communicate with my Spanish ELLs (English Language Learners)!

So this was another of my desires—obviously from Him (and another strong sign of that is, if we desire to do something (never against the Word, and something that will benefit us and others in good ways) and that desire persists year after year after year, then it is almost always a desire He has given us, and He will help us take steps to make it happen.

It was a blessing to be able to use the basic Spanish I knew, and I actually could tell that my Spanish English Language Learners—who really spoke no English at all, and were thus silent, listening and watching, and taking it all in—were understanding my basic Spanish (not just my TPR (Total Physical Response, meaning using hand signals, facial expressions, body language, etc.)) and obeying me.

Of course, I also used small whiteboards and the books and held them up to the camera, to demonstrate what I wanted. But some things were them replying to my spoken (in Spanish) commands. Also, several of my students were bilingual, and understood both languages. Only our sweet, loving Father could coordinate such a Blessing! The kids were blessed because I was using both languages, and I was blessed too. God always constructs a "win-win"!

Good teaching is continual improvement of processes, and the LORD gave me more ideas the weekend before the third week: To also write the expectations for the class, which I'd posted on the wall behind me so we could quickly review them at the beginning of every class, in Spanish. That way, the Spanish ELLs could see both languages at once, which is a tool that helps me learning Spanish, in some cases.

He also led me to do this with the class affirmation—"I am excellent—every day, every way!" (*Soy excelente, todos los días, en todos los sentidos!*) I had started out with several affirmation statements, but not only did that take too much time at the beginning of class, because I'd say one, then the class would say one, and sometimes we'd have to start over.

Or, as I tried later, I'd ask them to repeat the seven affirmations with me, but some would lag behind or go ahead, and with everyone's mikes on, it was just too distracting, and not synchronous enough to be effective. Plus, some of the more struggling readers (which included the two Spanish ELLs) were having a hard time following me.

So, dear Father God gave me the understanding to combine all of the affirmations (which come from the Bible, although they are not blatantly written as Scripture) into one, which covers it all. This is much more efficient, and works very well.

Also, now with a real need to use Spanish to help others, I was now super-motivated to quickly add more Spanish to my knowledge base. The LORD has helped me discover many excellent free resources. When I feel I've exhausted them, then I'll look into a paid course.

So I'm having a lot of fun, utilizing this delightful skill, and truly helping all the students to comprehend what I'm teaching—while, most of all, helping to understand I care for them and find them each unique and special! Also, before I teach each time, the LORD helps me remember to yield to Him, for He is the Master Teacher Who created each student and knows more than anyone what they need.

I rejoice that He puts His words in my mouth, and sometimes I am aware that He is leading me a new direction that I'd planned—but always exactly what those little ones need!

How great is our God! *(¡cuán grande es nuestro Dios!)_*

Happy Homeschooling: 17 Tips

1. Start with prayer, worship, and Bible study. This will help set your mind on things above, on the LORD. You may want to play praise and worship music in the background, or worship with your child(ren). Kids (of all ages) love to sing, and the LORD loves it when we sing His praise. He commands us in Psalm 100 to "enter His gates with thanksgiving and enter His courts with praise," and He Who is the Spirit of God lives in our praise!

2. Have everyone eat a good breakfast. The first meal of the day is very important. Be sure to include healthy proteins. If you have a picky eater, at least get them to drink good milk or organic juice.

3. Encourage them and let them "teach" you. Have fun learning together. Remember they are eager to please you, so as they learn, let them repeat back to you things they are excited about. Then you can have them tell or show you whether you are saying or doing it right. When my daughter was in 5th grade learning to play the recorder, I asked her to teach me. Her persona changed and she stood up taller. This sense of confidence came over her, and she highly enjoyed teaching me, her mother, how to play!

4. Make time to go outside and play when the weather permits. Rules of public school may change where kids have no recess, but everyone needs fresh air and sunshine for at least a few minutes a day. Even pets need it, so how much more do your kids need and deserve it? We feel better when we get light and fresh air, and when kids can run and play and yell, they get out pent-up energy that needs to be released. It also helps relax them while potentially increasing focus.

5. Integrate subjects when possible with field trips. Even a trip to the grocery store can be a research lesson (finding and comparing products), a math lesson (figuring how much products will cost, and the cost per serving, etc.), and a reading lesson (reading the labels on the can, and signs in the store, etc.). Plan longer trips when you

can. You can go to the park and conduct science experiments, and to museums for history trips. (While there is a curfew and travel is discouraged because of the virus junk, you can find plenty of videos on the internet to research.)

6. Teach electives also, such as music and a foreign language. Again, there are many how-to videos on the internet on such subjects, or use your own experiences if you have such skills. Spanish is one of the easiest languages to learn, and the most prevalent in the USA, so it would be very practical for your child(ren) to learn. They will have to have a foreign language to graduate, in most states.

7. If you are not confident teaching your own children, you can access many online schools that can help them.

8. Most of all, help your children understand that, while you expect them to do their best, grades aren't everything. As I've told my daughter and many other students that I've taught in public and private schools, grades are only a measure of part of who they are.

9. Teach them now about having wisdom in finances. You may choose to let them earn an allowance, or just give them money for completing projects or doing an outstanding job on something. They are never too young to be taught to tithe, give offerings to your church or other ministries, and to save money. Help them learn to make choices that are wise when they want to purchase something.

10. If you are homeschooling more than one child, have them occasionally to help each other in buddies or small groups, or establish a regular pattern for them working together daily. It may be literal help, or just discussion of what they have learned. This is a very important thing that children are learning in public and private schools—to talk to and listen to each other, while respecting each other, even if their opinions differ.

11. Discuss current subjects with them. You could ask your child(ren) for their opinions on world issues that are happening now. You could also discuss any number of issues that are historic or

scientific, or even ask them for creative ways they would solve any kind of problem. For instance, my daughter and I

12. Let them record themselves—audio (voice only) or video (voice and picture). Most people enjoy hearing and seeing themselves recorded. This will help them especially in getting over the fear of public speaking. The earlier they conquer this, the better!

13. Have them write in their own personal notebook or journal every day. They can use this, especially when it's divided into sections, to keep notes on various subjects. It is also very helpful for them to have either a separate notebook for personal opinions they will write daily, or at least a section in the back of their main notebook, that they can trust you won't look at, unless they want you to. But you can encourage them to share what they think. Keeping a daily journal is very important for their writing, critical thinking, and summarization skills.

14. Take them to the library or let them download books online to read and do book reports. Again, this will be an excellent exercise that covers multiple facets—reading, writing to a form (book report), critical thinking/summarizing, and finally, reading aloud their report, to strengthen their enunciation and articulation, and confidence in speaking in front of others.

15. Join a local homeschool group that meets at least once monthly. Usually, there are events where everyone brings food and has games and other activities for the kids so they and you can socialize with other homeschooling families. There are also many groups online.

16. Be sure and let the kids drink water through the day, and you do the same. Water is more important than food, and drinking plenty of good water helps maintain good health, plus focus. It balances the body—which is mainly made up of water! (You could do a science project on this.)

17. Above all, remember always that you love each other. Psalm 126:7 (TPT) says, **"Children are God's love-gift; they are heaven's generous reward."**

If you don't get everything done that you, the teacher, planned to get done in one day, you can have a go at it the next day, or through the week. (Sometimes, as I quote I read years ago stated, "courage" is simply deciding to be content with what was accomplished one day, then rest and prepare for the next.)

I finally learned (after years of pressuring myself and not healthily) that no teacher I've ever worked with in public or private school always got everything accomplished that was on her lesson plan, nor did I in the years I taught in public school, and not in the two years I homeschooled my daughter, either.

But we made it, and she learned quite a bit. The time you are spending with your kids—even if it's forced homeschooling because of the virus or other negatives—can be a wonderful time of working together and getting to know each other more!

Enjoy!

12 Fun Edutainment Ideas

https://www.youtube.com/watch?v=e7YYaIRYZoY
I have no greater joy than this, to hear that my [spiritual] children are living their lives in the Truth.—3 John 1:4, AMPC

Having served as a teacher for over 35 years in church and other nonprofits—including many years teaching public school, as well as homeschool and private lessons, plus 5 years teaching kids online across the nation and in 8 other countries—I've seen many kids get bored even with a beloved movie.

A movie is usually a way for the adults to disengage and/or chill, while the kids are occupied, and I certainly understand that. Video games can teach them a few skills, but should not be used to just keep the kids out of our hair. So (to start a sentence with a conjunction; please don't tell my ELA students I did this!), why not use that time to sharpen their minds and teach them positive, useful, fun things—especially about God?

You can use these in your children's church groups—in conjunction with the regular lesson, or as something different. The church library would be best having a stationery place, however, You could teach the kids classification systems for books, and more, and how to choose books pertinent to their levels and higher (for you always want to encourage them to read at least some at levels higher than their current ones!).

Yes, it does take time and effort to plan activities and get the materials together. True, they are not always appreciated, and some may get bored with your most "engaging" activity, but much less so, usually, if they are enjoying participating.

Most smart kids want to be active, so here are 10 ideas to help you help them—and you'll have fun and may even learn some things yourself! At the least, you'll reinforce your knowledge as you reinforce theirs.

Maybe it's the teacher and the reader in me, but I've seen kids at church gatherings that went long, and other events get bored with a movie or something docile, even when it's time to settle down and go to sleep, with their jammies on and fave pillow, while waiting for their parents to get out of a conference that is several hours long.

They aren't allowed to play video games as a group at church, but they really want stimulation.

These ideas definitely help keep things lively, fulfilling, and positive, to the glory of God, and help the time pass quickly! My hope is that you can employ some of each of them, to the delight and enhanced education of your young ones!

(1)Provide a Christian library—lots of materials, from books to magazines to Christian comic books, calendars with Scriptures, and whatever else you can find. As one pastor stated, kids don't have "junior" Holy Spirit, but The Holy Spirit! There is so much negative junk that kids have access to now, why not put as many positive materials—especially about the LORD Jesus and how much He loves them, and how He's the coolest—*The Awesome God*—in front of them?

Even if you have to set the library corner/area up every time, it will be worth it. If you're super-organized (or even if you're not!), you can keep a list and allow the kids to take books home. No worries about most things being too "adult" for them (unless they are books on marriage or addiction, or other truly adult themes).

Some of the most important lessons I've learned came from me reading "adult" leadership books and such, written by God-fearing authors and other positive people (read: no cursing or other vulgarity; no traumatic stories; no witchcraft, etc.!)

Who is like You, O Lord, among the gods? Who is like You, glorious in holiness, awesome in splendor, doing wonders?—Exodus 15:11, AMPC

After all, God is not just awesome in Vacation Bible School, or on Sunday mornings! We want our kids to know that He is awesome every day, every night, every way—He is right!

Let me add that these activities do not have to be blatantly about God, but you can let the students know that the LORD is with us always—especially as He indwells us when we believe in Jesus Christ as our Savior and LORD—and that He cares about every detail of their lives; their educations; their interests; their joys, and every other part of their lives! Hallelujah!

Behold, the Lord's eye is upon those who fear Him [who revere and worship Him with awe], who wait for Him and hope in His mercy and loving-kindness,—Psalm 33:18, AMPC

Other ideas which I've basically used successfully with various groups and individuals (online and in person) and ages of elementary kids (in public school and otherwise), are these:

(2)Praise and worship moves, with dance steps, and flags, streamers, and/or praise veil rings. It's so easy for the kids to praise and worship the LORD with their bodies and these tools, most of which they can make themselves (Which can be yet another idea for meaningful edutainment!

"It's who you are and the way you live that count before God. Your worship must engage your spirit in the pursuit of truth. That's the kind of people the Father is out looking for: those who are simply and honestly themselves before him in their worship. God is sheer being itself—Spirit. Those who worship him must do it out of their very being, their spirits, their true selves, in adoration."—John 4:23-24, MSG

Several years ago, when I taught 4th grade English in public school, I bought each of my 48 students small USA flags to wave, as we sang along to the video of Lee Greenwood's "God Bless the USA."

I told them before we started that they were going to write an essay about how they felt and what they thought during the experience.

I could see how God was working, as His Spirit touched us in that public school classroom. I believe He helped us all realized more deeply to appreciate and honor our beloved USA, which the LORD God moved men to found, so we could freely worship Him and have and promote His Word! The LORD will be faithful to give you more neat ideas than these 12!

(3) Flash cards ("Around the world," where two students compete to answer the fastest, and the winner goes to the next student; preferably "around the world"—all the way through the group. The others often get excited and want to shout out the answers, but I ask them to think of the answer in their heads, and they can whisper it to a buddy, but not shout it out). You can use facts on the Bible, worship lyrics, English, math, science, and whatever the LORD leads you to.

(4) Funny poetry and animal jokes, tongue twisters—Teach them about poetic techniques, jokes, and alliteration, and help them make up their own.

(5) Board games, especially educational (something besides mindless rolling of the dice and counting spaces till they stop, unless they are preschool or K5), are really good. They can team up in pairs or small groups.

(6) Young writers workshop—brainstorming and writing techniques; group stories and poems and songs; encouragement about sharing their work to promote God's purposes, etc, **"And then God answered: "Write this. Write what you see. Write it out in big block letters so that it can be read on the run. This vision-message is a witness pointing to what's coming.'"**—-Habakkuk 2:2, MSG

(7) Reader's theater—Kids love this, and just about any God-oriented or other positive story or book or magazine excerpt will work. This is like the reading actors do, where they sit around and read the script before the filming starts. The kids sit or stand, and read the parts. They enjoy adopting funny or more mature-sounding voices to

do play the characters in the skit. Some may even want to write their own skits!

(8) Indoor competitions—with soft frisbees, balls, etc., but make sure they have room and won't get hurt

(9) Online games they can do as a group, if you have a big screen (Kahoot, Quizlet, IXL, even Kahn Academy (which goes all the way to college, and covers every core subject), this is a great way to entertain the group—and let even those not participating hear the correct answers.

(10) Read-a-Thon—They can read short texts and talk with buddies, then present the report or other info to the group; they can give clues and have the group guess what they read, etc.

(11) Book character charades—They love this. Buddies or small groups of four are best. You can assign them known characters or have them read an excerpt and act it out, try to guess the characters, etc.

(12) Vocabulary treasure hunt—Have them read short texts, especially Bible stories and other Christian works, and find the treasures! Let the older kids create treasure hunts for the rest!

Rhyming and Non-Rhyming Poetry

My heart overflows with a goodly theme; I address my psalm to a King. My tongue is like the pen of a ready writer.—Psalm 45:1, AMPC

As one who has written and published many poems, many of which could be considered songs, I like to teach my English Language Arts (ELA) students how to write both rhyming and non-rhyming poetry.

There are a few distinctive differences, and I will use excerpts from my own work to illustrate them. I really like water—especially the Spirit of God, Who is Jesus the Living Water!—-so I write a lot about it.

Here is an excerpt from a non-rhyming poem I wrote:

In the desert of my soul,
Your smile is rain
Your laughter a shimmering pool
Amid the cool oasis of Your love.

Notice that the last word of each line does not rhyme with the last word on the line before or after it. This is a non-rhyming poem, but it still has rhythm and structure. The words evoke imagery that compares a desert (a "thirsty soul") to the refreshing, life-giving Water of the Word of God.

Here are the first four lines from my poem, "Water is a Living Thing":

Water is a living thing,
A necessary brook or spring;
All its fountains lithe and living,
Ever moving, ever giving...

Here, every last syllable rhymes with the last syllable of the line before or after it. Also, "giving" and "living" rhyme with one another.

Rhyming poems often use alliteration and assonance (internal rhyme), but the only required thing to create a "rhyming poem" is to make sure the last syllable of every other line rhymes, or every line with its mate, in a couplet.

Enjoy and share and may this enhance your pleasure and that of your students' too!

JESUS IS LORD!

Bonus #1: 7 Free Online Study Tools

And my God will liberally supply (fill to the full) your every need according to His riches in glory in Christ Jesus.—Philippians 4:19, AMPC

Father God is so good! He is the Master Teacher, to Whom I yield daily, before I teach my classes. He has revealed many fun and helpful sites that have increased variety and engagement for myself, as I studied for professional exams, and have taught many students many things.

I served several years teaching in public school, then started teaching online before the virus hit. Now I'm teaching full-time, both virtually in public school classes during the day, and helping many individuals in their homes during the days and evenings.

If you're a teacher who's getting weary of the brick-and-mortar school, check out online teaching! Just today, I was sent a grid of 500 new students waiting for tutors. This is just one company out of many in the US and beyond!

The online platforms I use have the capacity to screen share, and also to upload documents. This is extremely important, and allows a good variety of materials for you to use to keep your students (and yourself!) engaged for greater learning.

There are so many out there, that it would take you a while to explore them all. However, these are excellent and work well for me. I believe almost any student (adults included!) would benefit from them:

KahnAcademy.org - This nonprofit site offers help for K5-college, on math, science, ELA. There are online exercises with short videos, practice sets, and all shared step-by-step, making the lessons very easy to understand. Students can rack up points, and every success is celebrated!)

Quizlet.com - This site changes daily, because people all over the world use and create study sets for this site. You can find study sets in many languages, on the core subjects, languages, and all kinds of things, including professional exams. Quizlet offers matching games, flashcards, and other ways to test oneself. Some of the flashcards have pictures and audio. It's totally free, although there is a higher paid level in which you can enroll.

KidsNationalGeographic.com - This site has heavy graphics, and many facts and mini-movies on animals; personality quizzes; and other interesting things for kids of all ages.

Grammar-Revolution.com - This multi-page site has everything most of us would ever want to know about English and grammar! Mrs. Elizabeth, the webmaster/teacher, is very helpful and responds to personal questions by email within a few days. Even as an English teacher, I've learned some things from her about English that I don't remember learning elsewhere!

Commongroundinternational.com/free-learning/ - This site teaches Spanish for educators, students, and anyone else wanting to learn Espanol, or to improve their Spanish. There are many free materials and YouTube videos. I just discovered it a couple of days ago, and it's already been very helpful for me with my (primarily) Spanish-speaking students.

Engoo.com - This site has many categories and articles for English Language Learners, for both kids and adults.

Kahoot - I have used this a bit in the past, but it can be a bit complex to get going. It is neat that it can be set up for several players to be able to answer questions, with a timer.

If you need or want more, just "Google it" and the LORD your Good Shepherd will lead you to additional materials, that will be just right for you and your students!

He cares about every detail, and remember—He is the Master Teacher. When you yield to Him, He puts His Grace all over everything, and you connect even better with your students and families, and the instruction flows even better (and in more surprising and creative ways, I've found!), than if you just try to do it yourself!

Every student is precious, and the LORD will be faithful to lead you and connect you with just those students He knows only you can reach in the best way.

14 For all who are led by the Spirit of God are sons of God. 15 For [the Spirit which] you have now received [is] not a spirit of slavery to put you once more in bondage to fear, but you have received the Spirit of adoption [the Spirit producing sonship] in [the bliss of] which we cry, Abba (Father)! Father. 16 The Spirit Himself [thus] testifies together with our own spirit, [assuring us] that we are children of God.—Romans 8:14-16, AMPC

The LORD is our best Friend and God is our Father (when we have received Jesus Christ the LORD as our Savior and LORD by believing in what He did on the cross over 2,000 years ago to cleanse us of our sins by shedding His pure blood to pay the sin debt, that is!), and loves to help us.

While we were yet in weakness [powerless to help ourselves], at the fitting time Christ died for (in behalf of) the ungodly.—Romans 5:6, AMPC

Every child is precious in His sight, and He created and knows them perfectly, so He alone knows how they learn best.

How precious is Your steadfast love, O God! The children of men take refuge and put their trust under the shadow of Your wings.—Psalm 36:7, AMP

Also, as you build their trust and confidence in you; as they know that you really care for them (I tell my students soon and often that I pray for them, and that I am a Christian and ask the LORD to help me help them.), the LORD will open opportunities for you to brag on Him, and let them know He sees them, loves them, and wants to help them in every part of life!

And how from your childhood you have had a knowledge of and been acquainted with the sacred Writings, which are able to instruct you and give you the understanding for salvation which comes through faith in Christ Jesus [through the leaning of the entire human personality on God in Christ Jesus in absolute trust and confidence in His power, wisdom, and goodness].—2 Timothy 3:15, AMPC

He will instruct you and guide you in the way you should go; the way(s) to help them grow in confidence and succeed!

I [the Lord] will instruct you and teach you in the way you should go; I will counsel you with My eye upon you.—Psalm 32:8, AMPC

Yes, the God of Heaven will give you (and your students) success (Nehemiah 2:20)!

Bonus #2: Are You a P.O.W.E.R Writer?

https://www.youtube.com/watch?v=g36v9sHBfE0

And the Lord answered me and said, Write the vision and engrave it so plainly upon tablets that everyone who passes may [be able to] read [it easily and quickly] as he hastens by.—Habakkuk 2:2, AMPC

There are writers, and then there are *P.O.W.E.R* (Purposeful Operations With Eternal Rewards) Writers.

There are almost innumerable people who called themselves "Christian," and write and publish things are either not true to the Word of God, and can thus deceive readers who are truly seeking to know the LORD better, and/or publishing things that are full of carnal, emotional, even sexual pulls and other ideas that can misrepresent Christ and distract the reader(s) from Him.

Writing true to the Word—being a true P.O.W.E.R Writer—is a big responsibility, and a mandate from the Most High (I am preaching to myself first!).

Which one are you? Here are tips on how to know!

P.O.W.E.R (Purposeful Operations With Eternal Rewards) Writers:

(1) Read the Word, pray, and stay in attitude of worship and thankfulness to God daily.

(2) Know that (as God had to teach me!), the LORD expects us to use the gift of writing to "share the wealth" of His Word so others will know Him! It's not pride; it's humility!

He is the Author, and we His royal scribes (Matthew 13:52)! Just like He used people to write the Bible, when we write words breathed by the Holy Spirit, all the glory goes to Him.

(3) Even when writing fiction, keep the focus on the LORD, and stay true to His Word, even while broaching sensitive and subjects that might cause conflict. In other words, although some characters shown true to life may curse, there is really no need to put those foul words in

the work of a P.O.W.E.R Writer! (Just like Sherwood Baptist Church can produce such excellent movies like Facing the Giants, Fireproof, The Prayer Room, and more—with no distasteful cursing, sexual inferences, etc. If they can do it in movies, so can we in writing!)

We are all in process to become more like Christ (when we are sincerely seeking Him, of course, and His Spirit helps us desire and do that!).

Ask the LORD to help you by yielding to His all-knowing Holy Spirit, then trust that He is guiding you! I've had to overcome doubt myself, with some of the intense emotional things God has given me (but they've not gone against the Word, and they always pointed to the redemption and merciful grace of God!).

Let us practice to become more of a P.O.W.E.R (Purposeful Operations With Eternal Rewards) Writers and share the wealth of God's Word, to help many more know Him, for Jesus is coming soon!

JESUS IS LORD!

Bonus #3: Butterfly Story Poem

Mariposa made a flight

Upon a gentle zephyr;

She came unto a house of light

And there her new friend met her.

She brought the birthday girl delight

By helping her to see

That each of us do shine so bright

As we're meant to be.

So know always that Elohim

Created you in love;

And that you are His treasure and

He sees you from above.

Know now that you are a gift

To everyone you know—

And that you are an *objet d'art**

Everywhere you go!

*Work of art; masterpiece

(This poem accompanies "The Butterfly Story" on FaithWriters.com. See the following "vocabulary word find" for the story, and here's the audio story online: https://www.youtube.com/watch?v=eKP8LlTx_Bw Enjoy!)

Bonus #4: Butterfly Story Word Find

©2013 by Tonja K. Taylor

Help your students to expand their vocabulary, as they count the rhythm of the words and enjoy the rhyme.

They can find the words from "The Butterfly Story" at the link below: **https://articles.faithwriters.com/reprint-article-details.php?article=44794**

They can work on their own, or, if you think some of these words may be a bit overwhelming to them, have them get with a buddy, or in a small group, and talk about what they mean.

They can look them up in (a hardback, "real book") dictionary, or try to guess what they mean as they discuss them.

English words to find:

flight
house
light
friend
birthday
delight
helping
shine
bright
meant
know
always
created
love
treasure
above
gift
everyone

everywhere

Words from languages other than English:

Elohim (Hebrew: "**El** oh heem")

Mariposa (Spanish: "Mah ree **po** sah")

zephyr (French: **zeph** ur"),

objet d'art (French; "ohb zhah **dahr**")

God bless you and your students, and for all the ways you are a positive force in the earth!

Other Works by Tonja K. Taylor

P.O.W.E.R. Girl Adventures, Books I-V (soon available on Barnes
and Noble Amazon, and several other channels)
The New Legacy Expanded
Spirit Songs and Stories Enhanced
Spirit Songs and Stories 2
Visions of the King: Jesus Revealed
Your Holy Health: Effective Secrets to Divine Life
<u>Upcoming books:</u>
The Righteous Bride
Psalm Something
Soul Dance: The Art of the Worship of God
How to Grow Sonflowers (Children's devotional)
Properties of Light (a novel)
Water: Life!
You Are Safe With Jesus

Don't miss out!

Visit the website below and you can sign up to receive emails whenever Tonja K. Taylor publishes a new book. There's no charge and no obligation.

https://books2read.com/r/B-A-HSCAB-MKMHG

BOOKS 2 READ

Connecting independent readers to independent writers.

About the Author

Tonja K. Taylor loves to share the Good News of Christ, the Master Teacher, through books; media (You Tube: River Rain Creative, and POWERLight Learning, RainWater podcasts); online courses; author-in-school visits and other presentations; the POWERLightLearning website (upcoming end of May 2025); tutoring online; and serving in church, community, and across the world as God leads. She and her husband live to glorify the LORD in every part of life.

19 For just as by one man's disobedience (failing to hear, heedlessness, and carelessness) the many were constituted sinners, so by one Man's obedience the many will be constituted righteous (made acceptable to God, brought into right standing with Him). - Romans 5:19, AMPC

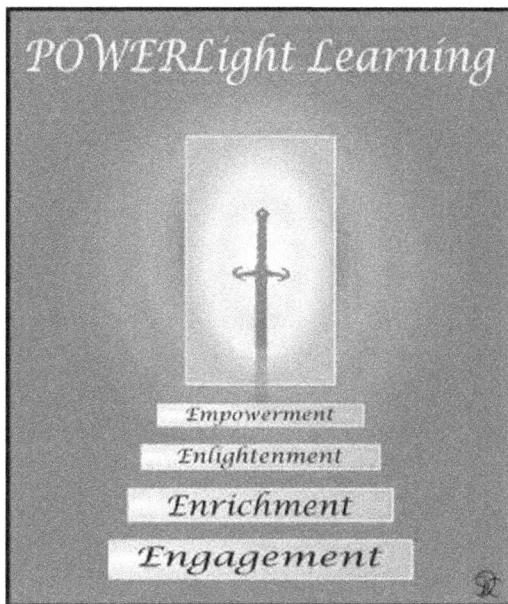

About the Publisher

Through engagement and enrichment comes enlightenment and empowerment—for bad or for good.

The book publishing arm of POWERLight Learning is based on Romans 5:19 and 12:2, and engages, enriches, enlightens, and empowers readers through positively provocative works for good, for God; *"Because what you read matters!"*

As the eternal, infallible, unchanging Word of God states: *"**For the kingdom of God consists of and is based on not talk but power (moral power and excellence of soul)."** -* I Corinthians 4:20, AMPC

It is our prayer that works by POWERLight Learning will draw all who experience them to a deeper love and loyalty to the LORD Jesus Christ, our soon-returning King!

Read more at https://www.faithwriters.com/member-profile.php?id=64826.

www.ingramcontent.com/pod-product-compliance
Lightning Source LLC
Chambersburg PA
CBHW022122280326
41933CB00007B/508